AF328595

30-SECOND
GREAT ART

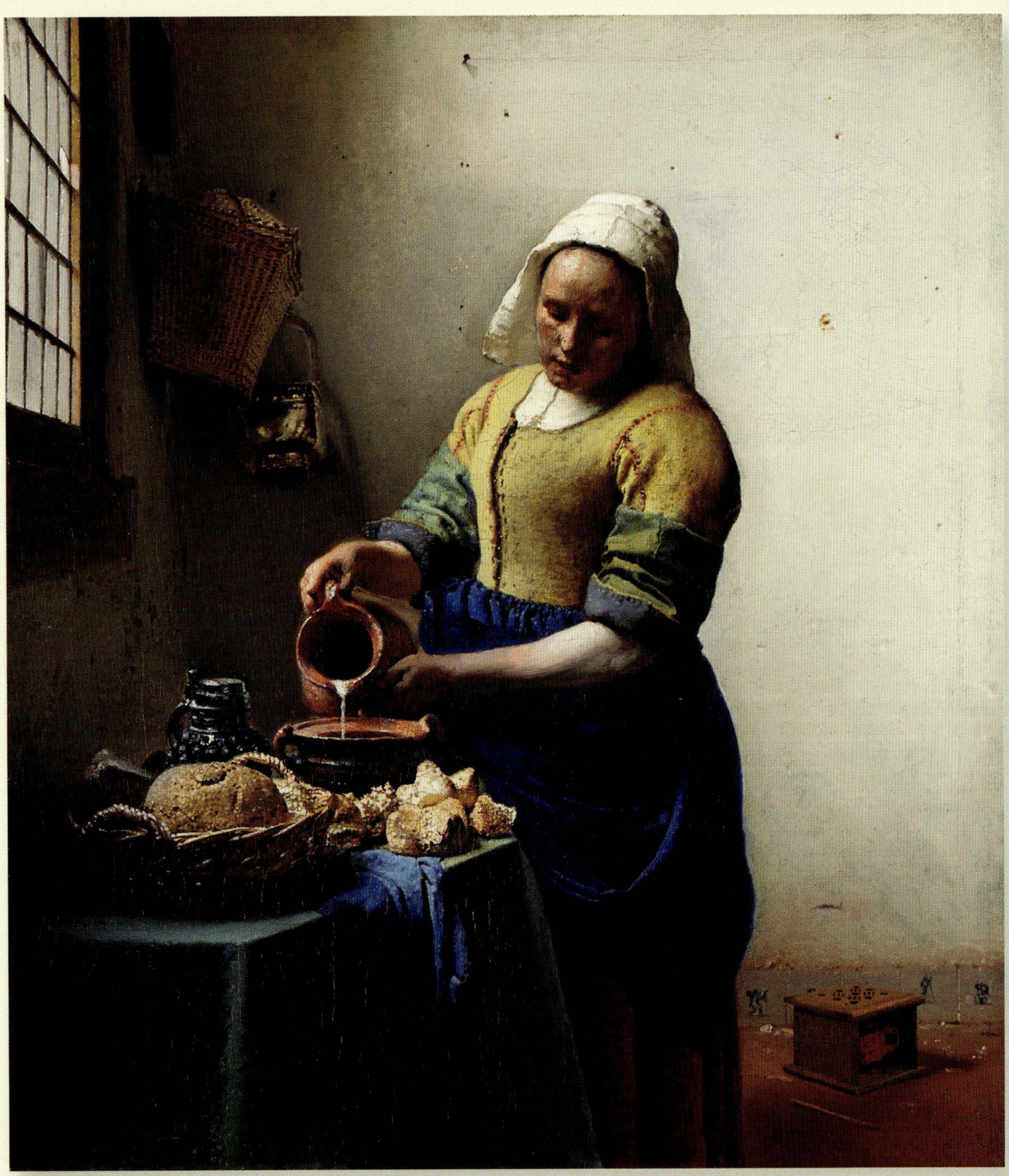

30-SECOND
GREAT ART

From Giotto to Warhol,
50 artworks that changed
the way we see things

Editor
Lee Beard

Contributors
Maria Alambritis
Thomas Balfe
Simona Di Nepi
Elena Greer
Paul Harper
Sarah Moulden
David Trigg

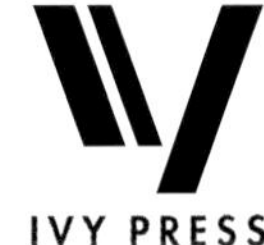

IVY PRESS

First published in the UK in 2018 by
Ivy Press
An imprint of The Quarto Group
The Old Brewery, 6 Blundell Street
London N7 9BH, United Kingdom
T (0)20 7700 6700 **F** (0)20 7700 8066
www.QuartoKnows.com

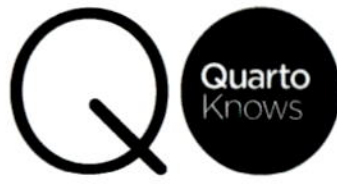

British Library Cataloguing-in-
Publication Data
A catalogue record for this
book is available from the
British Library.

ISBN: 978-1-78240-552-8

This book was conceived,
designed and produced by
Ivy Press
58 West Street, Brighton BN1 2RA, UK

Publisher **Susan Kelly**
Creative Director **Michael Whitehead**
Editorial Director **Tom Kitch**
Art Director **James Lawrence**
Commissioning Editor **Sophie Collins**
Project Editor **Joanna Bentley**
Designer **Ginny Zeal**
Picture researcher **Katie Greenwood**

Printed in China

10 9 8 7 6 5 4 3 2

CONTENTS

INTRODUCTION
Lee Beard

For as long as there has been a human need to create, communicate, make a mark or tell a story, there has been art. From the prehistoric cave paintings of Lascaux to the digital installations of the twenty-first century, the desire to capture ideas and events and present them as image or form has shaped civilizations across the globe. Like the spoken or written word, art has played an active role in the way societies have functioned, disseminating religious doctrines and political ideals, shaping national identities and creating shared mythologies that bind people together. At its finest it has stirred deep emotions, provoking feelings of joy, beauty and wonderment.

Taking into account the limitations of a modest-sized publication, and absent of any qualitative judgement regarding artworks from other eras or regions, the great paintings and sculptures in this book all emanate from a particular western tradition in art. Spanning the period from the early fourteenth century to the present day, the tradition is founded on the notable artistic achievements of the European Renaissance and the concomitant rise of a Humanist view of art. Although Christian subject matter still dominated during its early stages, as is evident in the paintings in the opening chapters of this book, the stylized heaven-bound saints and angels of the Middle Ages were already being replaced with more individual and naturalistic depictions of religious figures.

Over the following century, the position of the Church as the main patron of the visual arts gradually diminished, and the new largesse of the mercantile and aristocratic classes enabled artists to engage with a wider range of themes. As we can see with the two kneeling figures in Masaccio's *Holy Trinity*, patrons sometimes wanted to be included in the artworks that they had commissioned, in this case as a sign of their devotion and potential proximity to God. In turn, new types of secular patronage engendered a demand for forms of portraiture that would convey the power, wealth and status of the sitter, as is clear in the arrangement of objects and finery in Holbein's *The Ambassadors*.

The gentle affection shown between the Madonna and Child brings the religious figures closer to the everyday life of the viewer. Madonna of Humility *by Fra Angelico (1395-1455).*

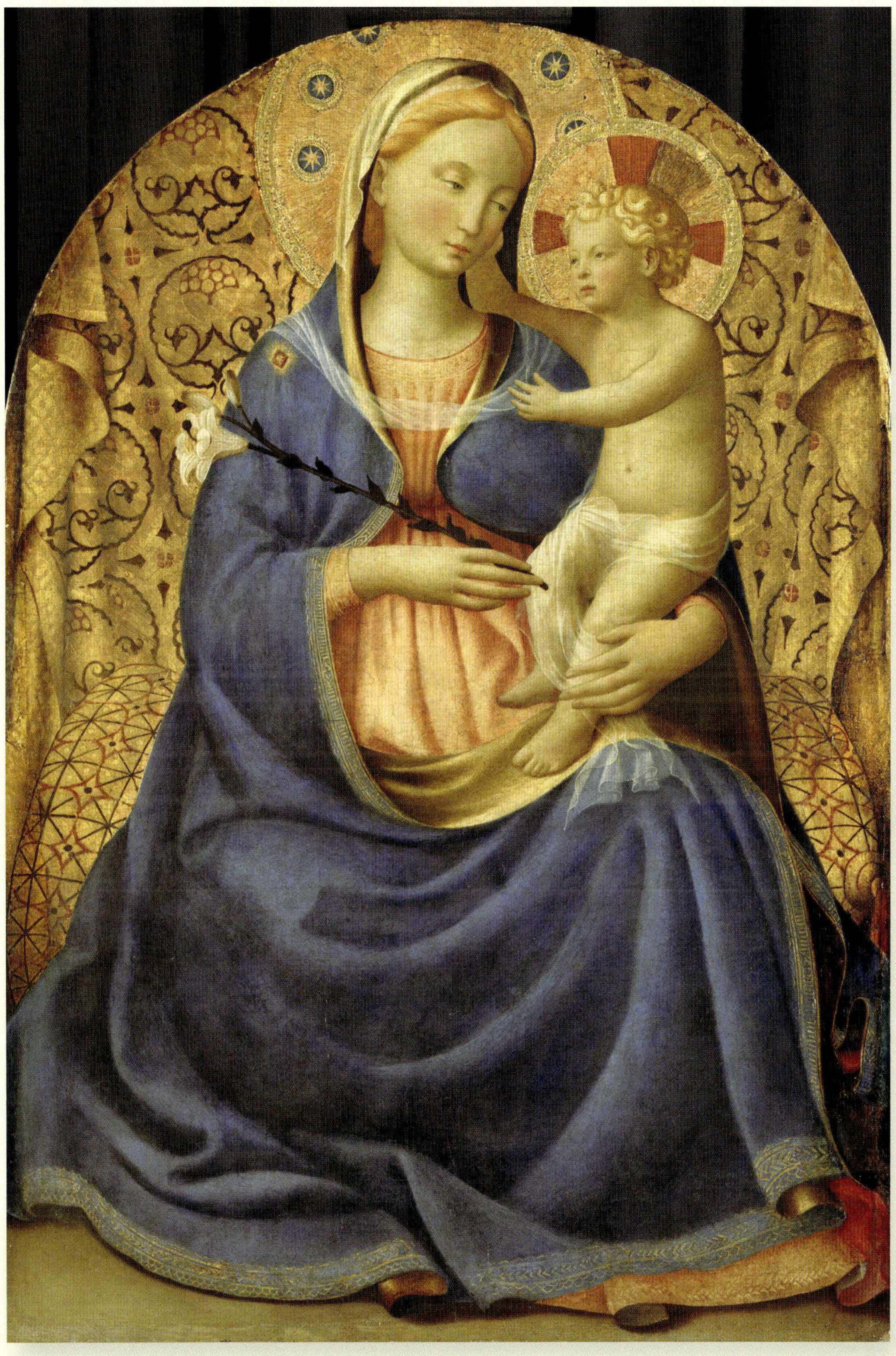

By the nineteenth century, with the rise of the Salon exhibition and the support of private dealers, artists found themselves in a position of even greater freedom, and the modern concept of artistic genius was firmly established. To a certain extent the groundwork had been laid five centuries earlier with Giotto. In contrast to the anonymous artisan, the Renaissance had witnessed the rise of the individual artist – their paintings often distinctive in style and technical mastery; their lives recorded by historians and biographers; and, for some, their work so highly prized it brought them fame and fortune. As the selection of paintings and sculptures here shows, across the centuries artists have continued to assert their own unique presence through their work. Whether through a gestural brushstroke or an innovative use of materials or, most explicitly, in the frankness of a self-portrait, the unequivocal link between artist and artwork is what has shaped this tradition.

How this book works

This book presents 50 great works of art divided into seven period-defined chapters. Alongside a full-page illustration, a 3-second sketch introduces each painting or sculpture, with a more detailed overview provided in the 30-second artwork text. Further contextual material is found in the 3-minute study, while the 3-second biographies introduce the reader to an important individual, or individuals, linked to the artist or artwork.

The opening chapter, **Renaissance: Part 1**, presents iconic paintings from the early Italian and Northern Renaissance. Dating from the fourteenth and fifteenth centuries, the technical and aesthetic advancements of this period shaped art for many centuries to come. Remarkably covering a mere four decades, **Renaissance: Part 2** contains some of art history's biggest hitters, including Michelangelo, Dürer and Titian. **Baroque & Beyond** highlights the great skill and mastery with which artists during this period

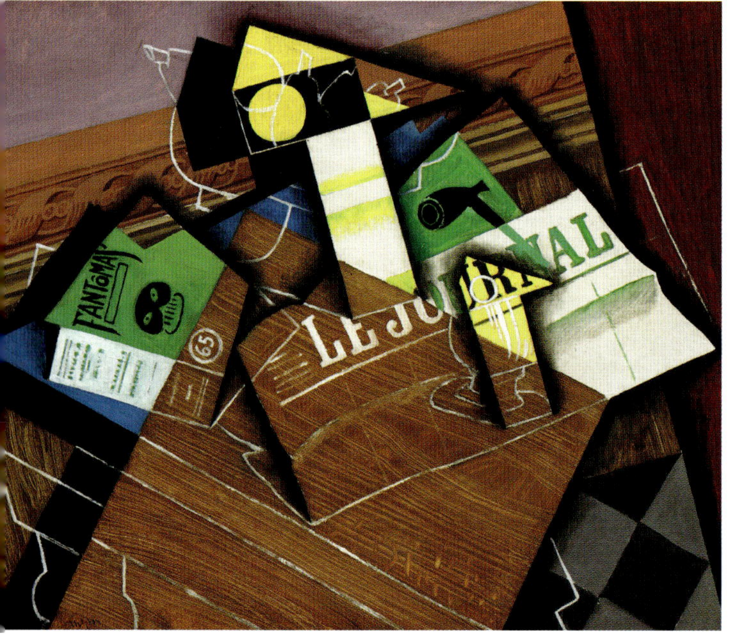

At different times through the centuries pictorial conventions in art were revised, revisited and, at times, rejected. Fantômas by Juan Gris (1887–1927).

succeeded in capturing in paint a wide range of human emotions and dramatic scenarios. Spanning the eighteenth and nineteenth centuries, **Neoclassicism & Romanticism** sees the rise of landscape as an important theme for artists, and also contrasts artists who looked to the past for inspiration with those who sought to capture the important events of the day. **Realism, Impressionism & Post-Impressionism** hints at the stylistic eclecticism and the preoccupation with the contemporary moment that would come to define modern art. This is followed by **Modernism**, beginning with the dawn of the twentieth century, when a series of radical avant-gardes broke down many of the established conventions of western art. The final chapter, **Post-war to Today**, reveals the ongoing expansion of the visual arts, in part the result of contemporary artists themselves constantly interrogating the inherent nature of art. It also indicates that the western tradition has become a truly universal one, ironically and perhaps inevitably at the point when the conventions of that tradition, not to mention the cultural assumptions under which it grew, no longer hold sway. Each chapter also includes a glossary of relevant art terms, plus a profile and timeline relating to a major individual or organization from that period.

In the hands of a skilful artist, landscape and portraiture could encapsulate beauty, status and social commentary in a single scene.
Mr and Mrs Andrews *by Thomas Gainsborough (1727-1788).*

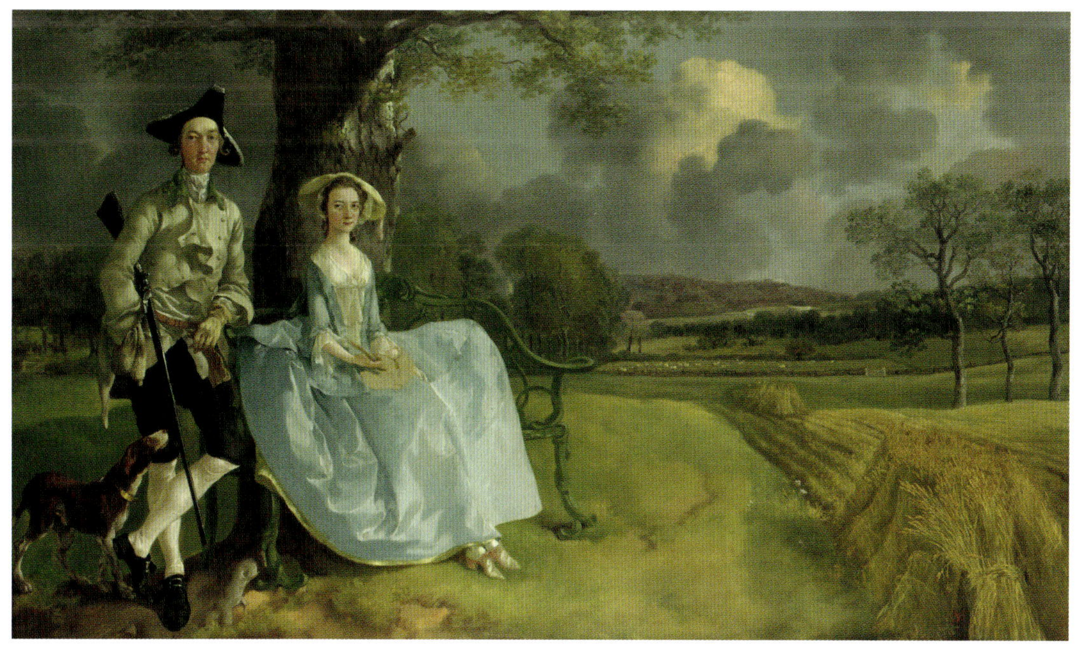

RENAISSANCE PART 1

antiquities Artefacts or buildings from ancient times. Usually originating from the Mediterranean regions dominated by Greek and Roman civilizations, and pre-dating the fifth century CE.

cameo A gemstone, shell or glass made up of two or more coloured layers that has been carved or moulded in relief. Usually small and intimate in size, and often integrated into jewellery, such as a brooch or pendant.

diptych A painting or relief comprised of two hinged panels. Depicting religious themes, these predominantly devotional objects could be folded shut to conceal or reveal the images at the appropriate time.

Early Renaissance Inspired by the Classical past, the Renaissance – or rebirth – began in Italy at the beginning of the fourteenth century. It was shaped by a growing awareness of humankind's pivotal position in the world and in the arts this led to a prioritizing of human anatomy and the development of perspective. The Early Renaissance period, from approximately 1300 to 1500, is typified by the works of Giotto and Masaccio.

fresco A wall or ceiling painting in which powdered pigment mixed with water is applied to wet lime plaster. On drying the painted composition becomes an integral part of the plaster. This technique is known as *buon fresco*, as opposed to *fresco secco*, where the pigment is applied to the plaster once it is dry.

memento mori Translated from Latin as 'remember you must die', a symbol in art intended to remind the viewer of the ephemeral nature of life. Common forms include an hourglass, skull or skeleton.

Middle Ages Period in European history from approximately the fifth to the fifteenth century. The term 'middle' derives from the fact that it covers the epoch between the fall of the Roman Empire and the beginnings of the Renaissance.

Northern Renaissance Relating to art and artists active in European countries situated north of the Alps during the fifteenth and sixteenth centuries, as distinct from the Renaissance in Italy and other southern European countries. Unlike their Italian contemporaries, Northern artists were less influenced by the Classical past.

oeuvre French word meaning 'work'. In art it refers to the complete body of work produced by an individual artist throughout his or her career.

oil paint Made by binding coloured pigment with an oil medium, such as linseed oil. Due to the richness, range and resilience of the colours, along with its slow-drying and reworkable nature, the development of oil paint in the fifteenth century was seminal to the development of western art.

Passion of Christ The Passion represents the events leading up to, and following the crucifixion of Christ. The distinct sequence of the narrative – including 'The last supper', 'Mocking of Christ', 'Descent from the cross' and 'Resurrection' – resulted in it becoming a popular theme in the decoration of religious buildings.

pathos Conveying a sense of sadness or pity.

patron An individual or organization that gives financial support to an artist. This can be by means of commissioning a single artwork, or assisting them over longer periods throughout their career.

perspective The convincing representation of a three-dimensional object, or spatial area, on a two-dimensional surface. In the early fifteenth century Filippo Brunelleschi (1377–1446) was credited with the invention of linear perspective, which would become the bedrock of western art.

portrait The depiction of a person in painting, drawing, sculpture or, in modern times, photography. As well as capturing a physical resemblance, throughout history portraits have been a means to convey the status or power of the individual represented.

sarcophagus A stone coffin that is often decorated with carvings and inscriptions.

tempera A type of paint made by mixing ground, coloured pigment with a water-soluble binder, usually egg yolk. Tempera was used in the painting of panels, manuscripts and murals. Unlike oil paint, which would replace it during the fifteenth century as the dominant medium, tempera is quick drying.

the 30-second artwork

This scene depicts mourners

weeping over Christ's body after its removal from the cross. Giotto has used a variety of gestures to express the pathos of the moment. Female mourners surrounding Christ hold up his limp limbs and his head, emphasizing the weight of his lifeless corpse. The Virgin Mary gazes sorrowfully at her son's face, which she holds close to her own as she embraces him. Mary Magdalene, recognizable by her long red hair and red dress, is seated at his feet, recalling the moment she showed that she recognized his divinity by washing his feet. By contrast, the disciple in the centre in pink – probably John, the beloved disciple – throws his arms back dramatically in anguish. Giotto emphasizes the cosmic nature of the event by echoing this gesture in the mourning angels who are shown, foreshortened, breaking into the scene. The two cloaked figures visible only from behind may be intended as ciphers for the viewers of the fresco; this invitation to identify with the scene reflects a strand of early fourteenth-century spirituality that encouraged Christians to engage emotionally with Christ's humanity and suffering. By rejecting the stock pictorial conventions used by his contemporaries and making the scenes more accessible to worshippers, Giotto reinvented the language of Christian iconography.

3-SECOND SKETCH
Giotto depicts an unprecedented range and depth of grief in the lamentation over Christ's body through solidly human figures with whom the viewer can identify.

3-MINUTE STUDY
This painting belongs to a series of frescoes depicting the life of the Virgin Mary and the life of Christ. These were commissioned to decorate the walls of a large private chapel, called the Arena Chapel, in Padua. Banker Enrico Scrovegni commissioned the chapel in 1300 as both a status symbol and a way to atone for his family's business of money-lending, a profession considered sinful in medieval thought.

DETAILS OF THE WORK
Fresco, 1305
231 x 236 cm (91 x 93 in)
Arena Chapel, Padua

3-SECOND BIOGRAPHY
ENRICO SCROVEGNI
d. 1336
The richest man in Padua at this time, whose father Reginaldo (d. 1288 or 1289) appears as the chief moneylender in the seventh circle of hell in the *Inferno* by Italian poet Dante Alighieri

30-SECOND TEXT
Elena Greer

The faint outlines of different sections visible in the background indicate giornata, *the amount of fresco that could be plastered and painted in a day.*

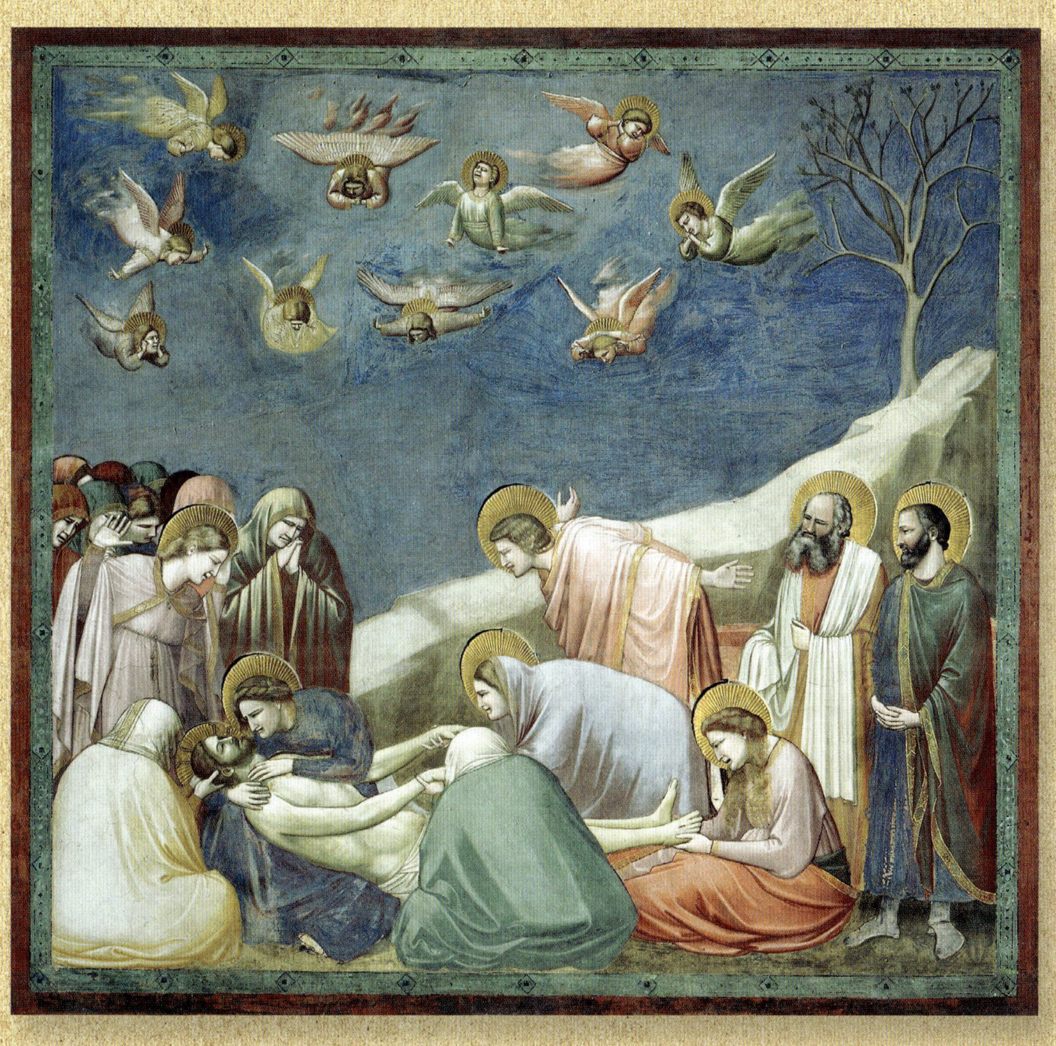

the 30-second artwork

Masaccio is arguably the most influential artist of Early Renaissance Italy. Despite his premature death, his unprecedented realism and pioneering use of linear perspective in painting had an immense impact on other artists. One of the most striking works is his burial fresco in Santa Maria Novella. In this funerary monument the artist painted a fictive, illusionistic chapel seemingly breaking into the church's wall. The monumental space features a brilliantly rendered barrelled vault, Ionic columns and Corinthian pilasters. Within the architecture the solemn figure of God the Father holds the crucifix on which hangs the dead Christ. Between their heads is the white dove, symbol of the Holy Spirit. Standing at the feet of the cross are the Virgin, on the left, pointing us to her son's sacrifice, and St John, on the right, mourning with his hands clasped. On the outside ledge the painting's patrons kneel in prayer. In the painted sarcophagus Masaccio cleverly inserted a memento mori, a reminder of the viewer's own mortality. It is a skeleton bearing the epitaph: *'Io gia ` fui quell che siete e quell che chio son voi sarete'* ('I was once what you are and what I am you will be').

3-SECOND SKETCH
In this bold interpretation of the Holy Trinity, Masaccio turns painting into architecture by giving the illusion of real, three-dimensional space.

3-MINUTE STUDY
In about 1420, Masaccio's friend Filippo Brunelleschi developed linear perspective, a mathematical method designed to reproduce three-dimensional reality on a two-dimensional surface. The technique, consisting of parallel lines converging on a single vanishing point in the distance, allowed Masaccio to give the astounding illusion of depth evident in the *Holy Trinity*, effectively creating a fictive chapel. He was the first painter to employ this method.

DETAILS OF THE WORK
Fresco, ca. 1426–27
667 × 317 cm (263 x 125 in)
Santa Maria Novella, Florence

3-SECOND BIOGRAPHY
FILIPPO BRUNELLESCHI
1377–1446
Florentine architect, engineer, sculptor and painter. Inventor of linear perspective, through which painters could give a realistic representation of the real, three-dimensional world

30-SECOND TEXT
Simona Di Nepi

The realistic likenesses of Masaccio's donors break with the generic representation of patrons that was typical of Italian religious paintings.

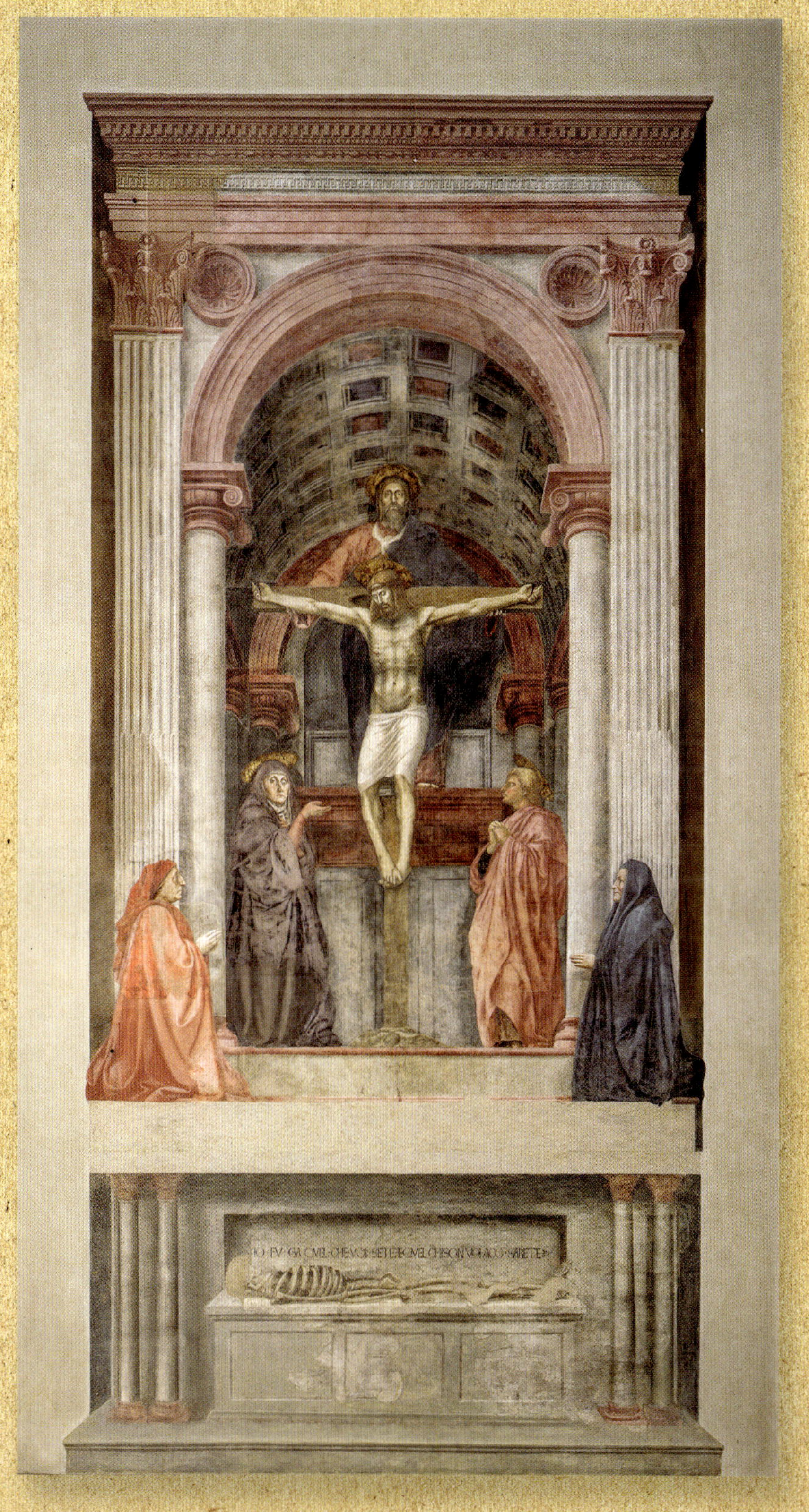
IO FV GIA QVEL CHE VOI SETE E QVEL CH I SON VOI ACO SARETE

JAN VAN EYCK
(Active from 1422; died 1441)

the 30-second artwork

Giovanni Arnolfini and his wife pose in the upper storey of a red brick house in the trading city of Bruges. They stand among an array of costly and carefully arranged objects, including a carved bed draped in scarlet fabric – an unusual and extravagant item for a living room. The chest beneath the window is scattered with exotic, imported oranges. The painter deploys a range of brushstrokes to describe the variety of textures on view, from the dog's silky coat to the dense, short fur that trims the couple's gowns. The portrait was once thought to commemorate the subjects' betrothal or marriage, but this is now considered unlikely. In turn, the woman's pose does not denote pregnancy, but instead reflects contemporary fashion. Four tiny figures are reflected in the circular mirror on the back wall. One is probably a miniature self-portrait of the painter himself; the elaborate Latin script above the mirror reads, 'van Eyck was here, 1434'. Van Eyck reworked the painting repeatedly, adding details such as the dog and the chandelier at the last minute. Such spontaneity suggests that the portrait may have been a gift from the artist to his friends; this might account for Arnolfini's raised hand, held up in a gesture of greeting.

3-SECOND SKETCH
Van Eyck marks his own presence in this double-portrait, full of carefully observed details showing off the wealth and taste of Italian merchant Giovanni Arnolfini.

3-MINUTE STUDY
A leading early figure in what is known as the Northern Renaissance, van Eyck was renowned for his skill in exploiting the full potential of oil paint to render texture and light effects in extraordinary detail. His surviving oeuvre is small but includes religious as well as portrait commissions, a genre usually reserved for rulers at this time. This picture may thus be the earliest surviving example of a double portrait in a domestic setting.

DETAILS OF THE WORK
Oil on oak, 1434
82.2 x 60 cm (32¼ x 24½ in)
The National Gallery, London

3-SECOND BIOGRAPHY
GIOVANNI DI NICOLAO ARNOLFINI
ca. 1400–after 1452
Worked in Bruges but came from a wealthy Italian merchant family from Lucca

30-SECOND TEXT
Elena Greer

The direction of the ceiling beams and floorboards leads the eye to the mirror in which the artist has depicted himself.

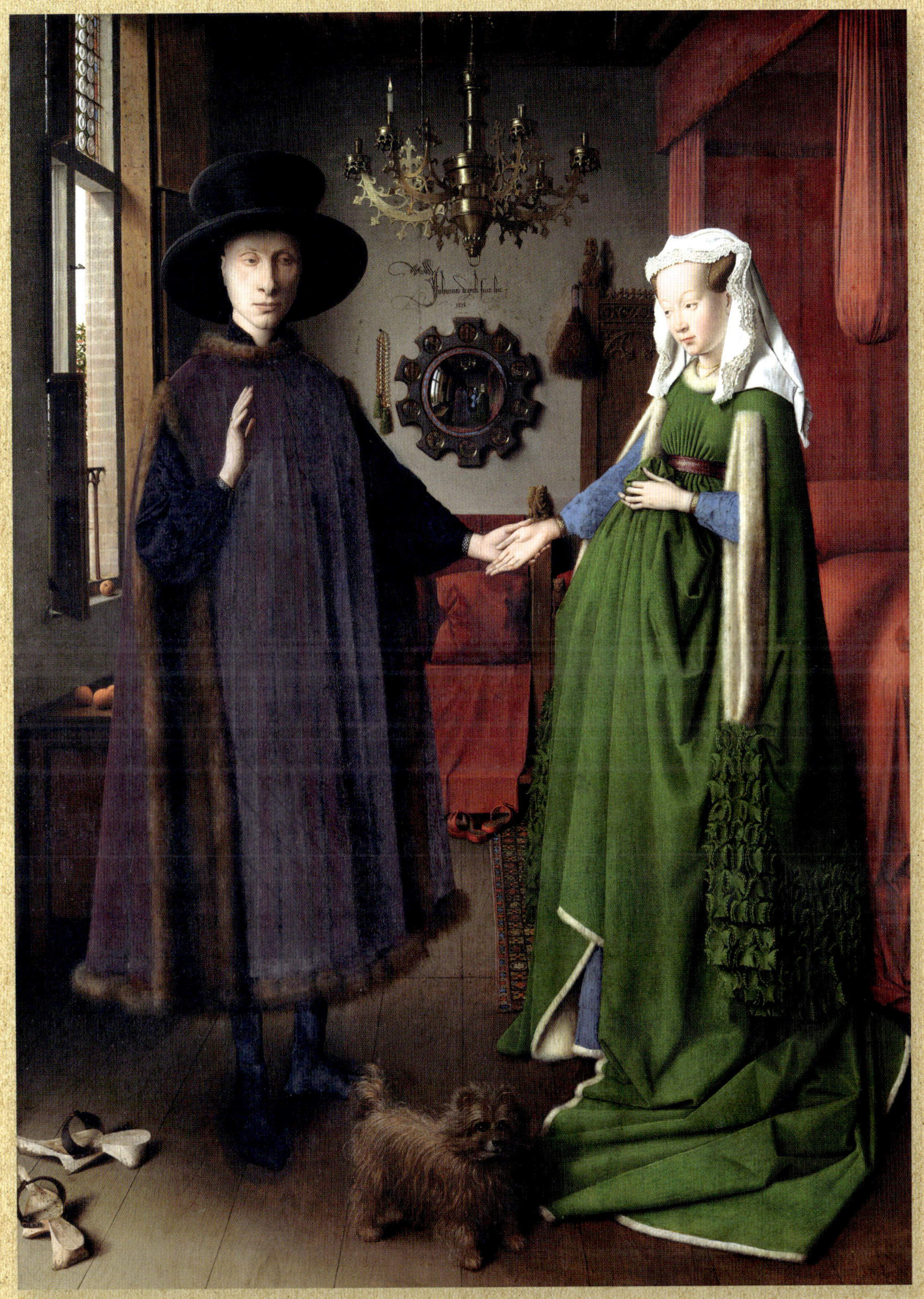

DUKE AND DUCHESS OF URBINO

PIERO DELLA FRANCESCA
(ca. 1415/20–1492)

the 30-second artwork

With this work, the Tuscan painter and mathematician Piero della Francesca created one of the most memorable portraits of the Italian Renaissance. The diptych represents the Duke of Urbino, Federico di Montefeltro, with his wife Battista Sforza, who died at 26 after giving birth to their seventh child. The couple is depicted in profile against a wide panoramic landscape. Piero adheres to the strict profile rule of fifteenth-century Italian portraits, which emulated classical portrait medals of emperors and generals. In such a way the painter cleverly disguises the Duke's loss of one eye, showing only his patron's 'good side'. Piero's close observation of details, inspired by Netherlandish pictures circulating in Italian courts, is evident in Battista's elegant attire and magnificent jewellery. The panoramic backdrop also echoes Netherlandish painting, while the landscape's misty quality, with the hills disappearing in the hazy distance, contrasts with the precise rendering of the donors. As shown by the Duke's nose, the profile view and fine clothing do not prevent Piero from retaining the verisimilitude of a credible likeness. Piero learnt the power of realism from Flemish Masters as well as from Masaccio, whose works he must have studied in Florence.

While not representing a specific place, the view suggests Montefeltro's territories, dropping down to the Adriatic.

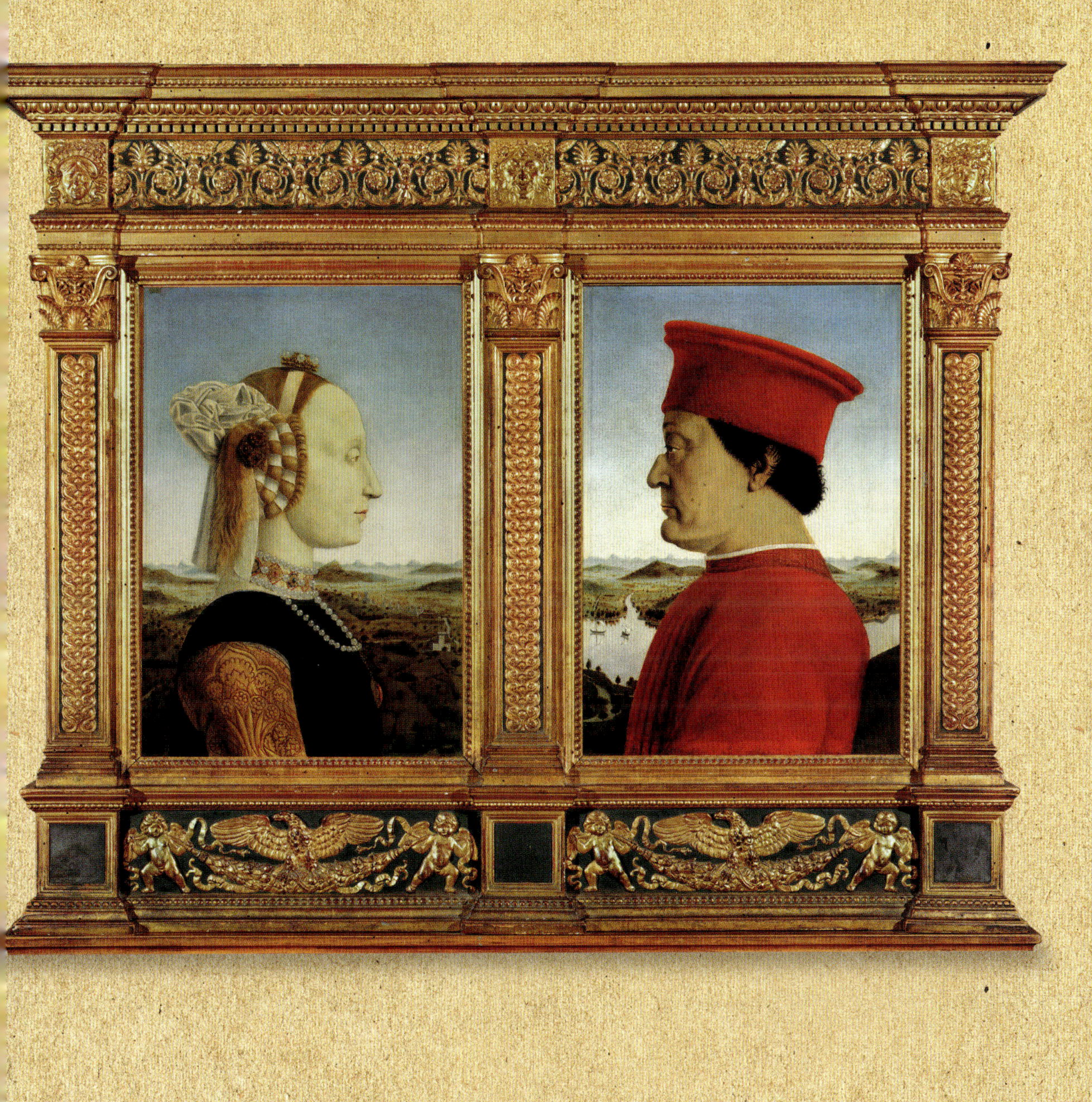

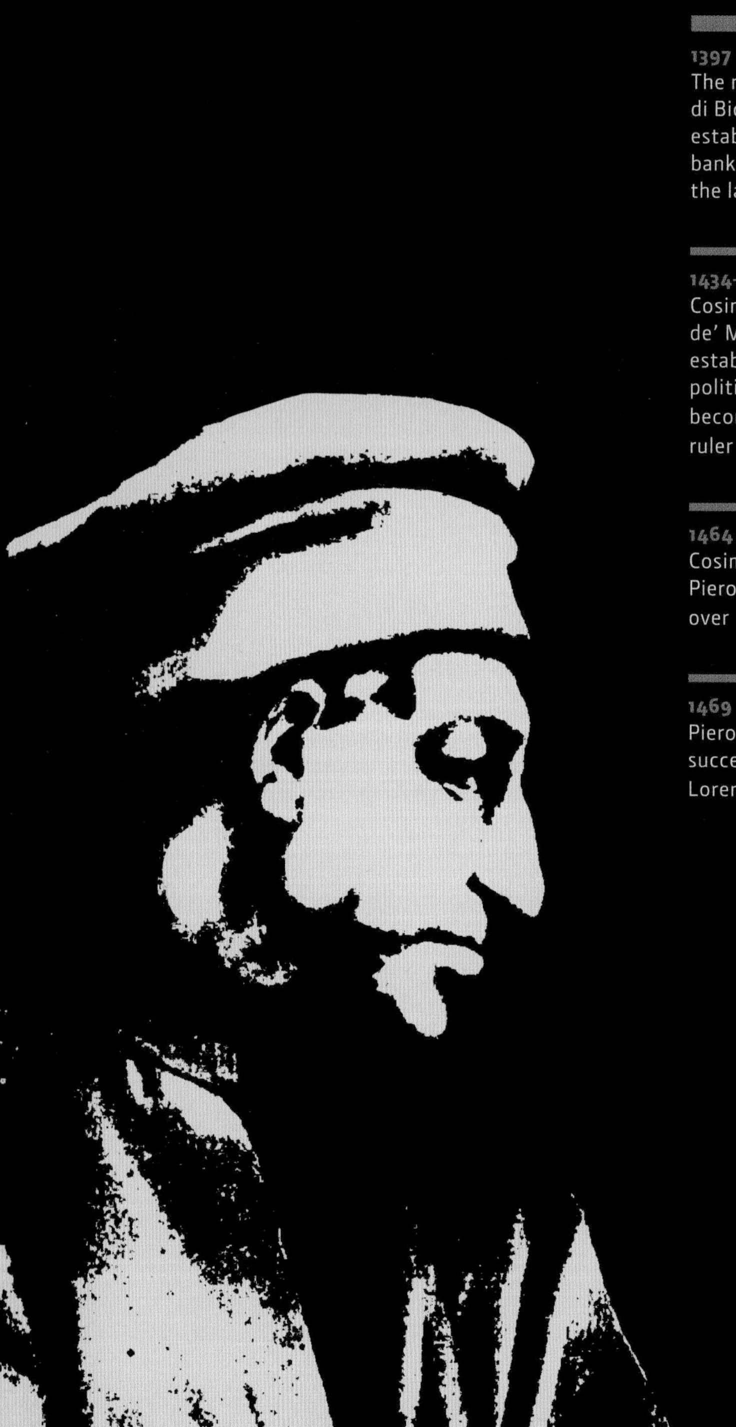

1397
The merchant Giovanni
di Bicci de' Medici
establishes the family
bank, which will become
the largest in Europe

1434–64
Cosimo di Giovanni
de' Medici 'the Elder'
establishes the Medici
political dynasty and
becomes the *de facto*
ruler of Florence

1464
Cosimo dies and his son
Piero 'the Gouty' takes
over

1469
Piero dies and is
succeeded by his son
Lorenzo 'the Magnificent'

1478
The Pazzi Conspiracy:
Lorenzo and his brother
Giuliano are attacked at
the Duomo during Sunday
Mass. Giuliano is stabbed
19 times and dies;
Lorenzo survives

1482
The Dominican friar
Girolamo Savonarola
begins preaching against
the Medici

1492
Lorenzo dies and his son
Piero 'the Unlucky' fails
to control the city.
Lorenzo's son Giovanni
(the future Pope Leo X) is
officially named Cardinal

1494
Piero de' Medici and his
brothers are expelled
from Florence and a
'popular republic' is
established. The Medici
will return to rule
Florence in 1512

THE MEDICI

A distinguishing trait of fifteenth-century art is the increased importance of private patrons, particularly those of the ruling elite. Whether commissioning altarpieces for their family chapels or domestic paintings for their sumptuous dwellings, these figures stood behind some of the greatest masterpieces of the Italian Renaissance. This phenomenon was epitomized by the Medici family of Florence.

Though in name Florence was a republic, the Medici, a wealthy banking family, controlled the city by placing their allies in government. Their rise to power began in 1397, when Giovanni di Bicci set up the first bank; his son Cosimo 'the Elder', established a political dynasty; then, after his son Piero's short rule, Lorenzo 'the Magnificent' carried his grandfather's legacy forward in both politics and art.

The leading architects, painters and sculptors of the time, including Brunelleschi, Botticelli and Donatello, all worked for the Medici. Michelangelo, who in the sixteenth century would embark on major Medici commissions, studied in Lorenzo's 'sculpture garden'.

Cosimo hired Michelozzo, his favourite architect, to rebuild the Dominican convent of San Marco and the painter Fra Angelico to adorn the walls of the friars' cells with frescoes of the Passion of Christ. Cosimo also entrusted Michelozzo with designing a sumptuous family palace, the Palazzo Medici, and filled it with paintings, sculptures and antiquities. Donatello produced two bronze statues of biblical heroes for the Palace: his naked *David* once stood in the courtyard while *Judith and Holofernes* was placed within the walled garden. A few years later, Benozzo Gozzoli was hired to decorate the Palace Chapel with spectacular frescoes depicting the *Procession of the Magi*, featuring portraits of the Medici family and their allies.

Lorenzo also appreciated small, precious objects: ancient cameos, vases, jewels and statuettes. A poet and scholar, he was also an astute politician who used art as a diplomatic tool. He sent gifts and encouraged others to employ his preferred artists and architects. Following the war between Florence and Rome, Lorenzo sealed peace negotiations by sending Sandro Botticelli, Domenico Ghirlandaio, Cosimo Rosselli and Pietro Perugino to paint the *Stories of Moses and Christ* on the walls of the Sistine Chapel.

After the turmoil following Lorenzo's death in 1492, and the expulsion of the Medici from Florence, the family's role in the arts resumed with their return in 1512. The sixteenth century saw further ambitious Medici commissions, such as Michelangelo's Medici Chapel and the Laurentian Library at San Lorenzo.

Simona Di Nepi

SAINT GEORGE AND THE DRAGON

PAOLO UCCELLO (ca. 1397–1475)

the 30-second artwork

This painting shows an episode from the life of St George, as told in Jacobus de Voragine's *The Golden Legend*, a book that served artists as a manual on the lives of the saints. In order to appease a hungry dragon, the inhabitants of Silene, in Libya, would feed it people, selecting victims by drawing lots. When the same terrible fate befell the king's daughter, St George saved her by piercing the dragon with his lance, before instructing the princess to use her girdle as a leash. Uccello compressed several moments of the story into a single scene. To a modern viewer, elements such as the grotesque dragon, simplified horse and schematic armour possess a cartoon-like charm. The gathering storm at the top right is symbolic of the unfolding drama. Although a religious subject, the picture's romantic courtly overtones and small size suggest it was made for domestic use, perhaps to hang in a young couple's bedroom. Uccello's works represent an unusual attempt to merge the fairy-tale imagery of the Middle Ages with the scientific innovations of Renaissance art, primarily mathematical perspective. These two, seemingly contradictory interests are seen in Uccello's most famous work, the *Battle of San Romano* trilogy, now divided between the National Gallery, the Louvre and the Uffizi Gallery in Florence.

Slender and fair, the third-century princess exemplifies the Italian Renaissance ideal of female beauty.

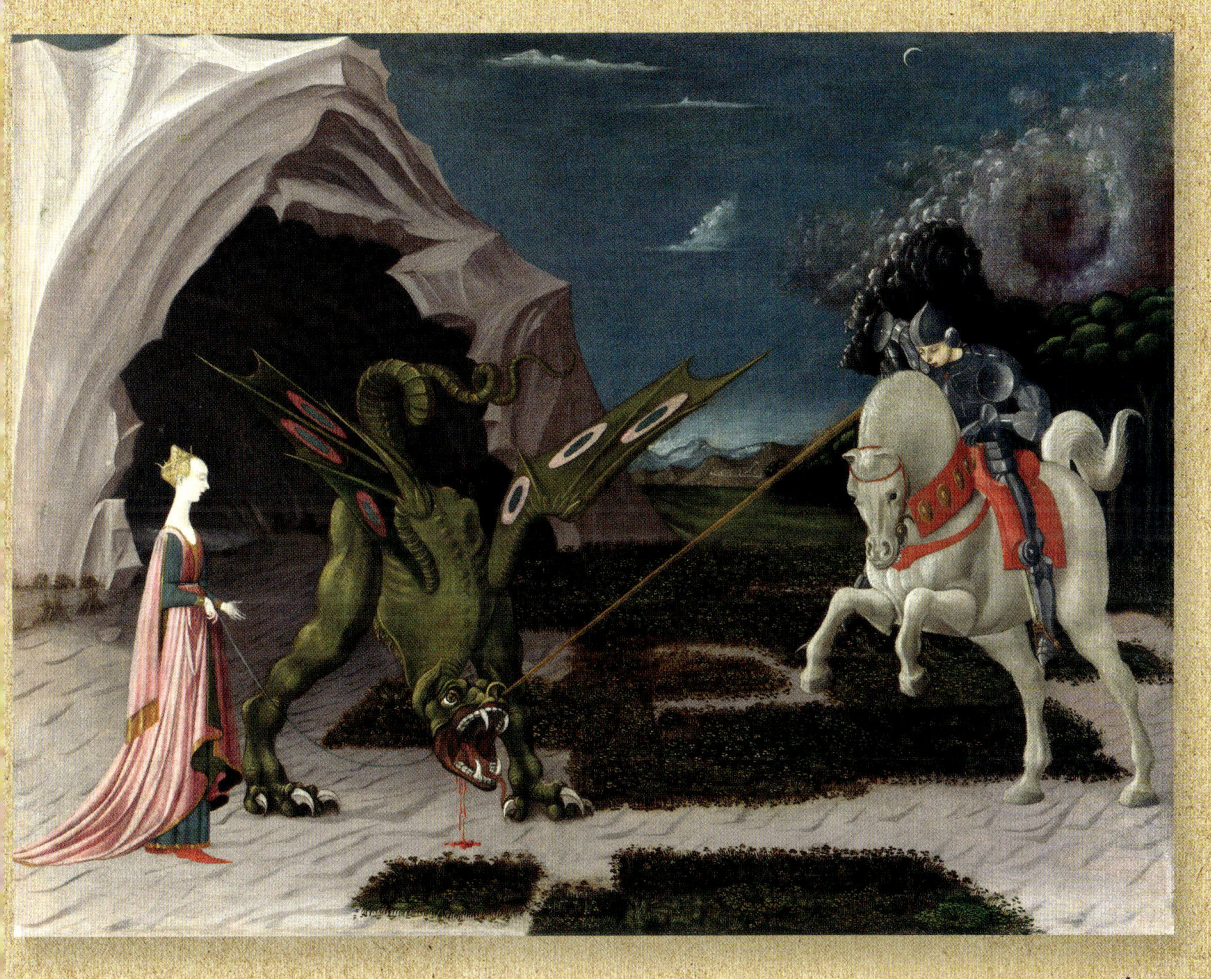

the 30-second artwork

The beautiful sitter is Cecilia

Gallerani, a young Milanese woman and poet who at the time this portrait was made was about sixteen years old. Cecilia, known both for her beauty and intellect, was the mistress of Ludovico Sforza, Duke of Milan. The fashionable sitter is seen holding an ermine. The furry animal is seen as a double symbol: of Ludovico because he used it as his emblem, after being bestowed the Order of the Ermine; and of Cecilia because the Greek name for ermine, *galee*, recalls her surname. Furthermore, in the Renaissance the weasel's whiteness was associated with purity and moderation, two virtues fit for a young woman. New scientific research has revealed that Leonardo only added the animal at a later stage, probably prompted by Ludovico or Cecilia herself. The portrait's allure lies in Cecilia's dynamic pose and intelligent gaze. As though someone has just entered the room, she turns to the left so that her head is opposite to her bust. Yet even in a moment of apparent distraction, Cecilia maintains her calm and dignified demeanour: her gaze is attentive yet unperturbed, her posture dynamic yet composed. Thanks to its exceptional sense of dynamism and its departure from the strict profile of female portraits, *Lady with an Ermine* has been acclaimed as the 'first modern portrait'.

3-SECOND SKETCH
This beautiful picture is pivotal to the history of female portraiture, with Leonardo eschewing the traditional profile to create a dynamic and compelling likeness.

3-MINUTE STUDY
Lady with an Ermine was painted while Leonardo worked as court artist for Ludovico Sforza in Milan. At this time Leonardo was exploring his many talents and interests: painting court portraits, executing *The Last Supper* and working on a huge clay model for the equestrian monument of Ludovico's father, among many other projects. In 1499, with the arrival of French troops and the fall of the Sforzas, Leonardo was forced to flee the city.

DETAILS OF THE WORK
Oil on panel, ca. 1489–90
54 x 40 cm (21¼ x 15¾ in)
Czartoyski Foundation, on deposit at the National Museum, Cracow

3-SECOND BIOGRAPHY
LUDOVICO SFORZA
1451–1508
Duke of Milan, ruthless prince and enlightened patron who, by employing artists, poets, architects, engineers and musicians, turned Milan into one of the most important European capitals

30-SECOND TEXT
Simona Di Nepi

The original background, of subtle differing tones, was overpainted in black during the nineteenth century.

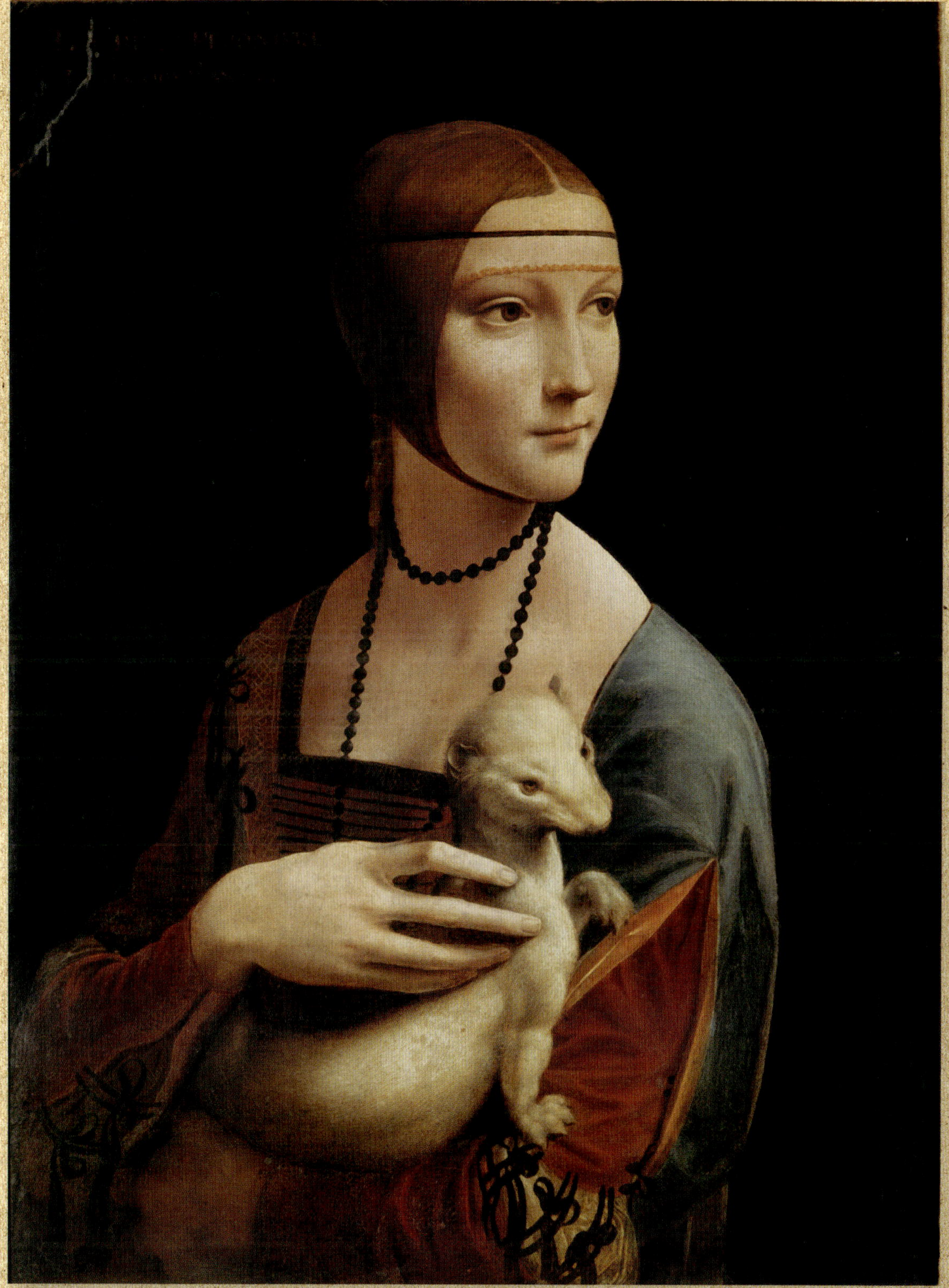

RENAISSANCE PART 2

altarpiece A Christian devotional painting
or sculpture positioned above or behind the
altar in a church, facing the congregation.
The religious imagery was often painted
on hinged panels (*see* triptych).

basilica An important Catholic church
based on the architectural layout of
Roman secular buildings from the second
century CE. The design of these semi-public
buildings, based around a central nave, was
first adopted for Christian worship under
the rule of Emperor Constantine in 312 CE.

cherubs / *putti* Small, winged children
shown in a heavenly realm. The term *putto*
(plural *putti*) is specifically applied to a
chubby naked boy, not necessarily winged.

Classical Dating from ancient Greece
and Rome, or later examples of art and
architecture that conform to the style and
examples of these periods. Characterized
by order, balance and clarity, the Classical
model has remained a major source
of reference throughout the history
of western art.

contrapposto A representation of the human
form that positions the body in such a way
that the upper and lower parts of the body
are orientated to face slightly opposing
directions to create a sense of asymmetry
and balance. Its development in the statues
of ancient Greece was a major contribution
to a greater naturalism in art.

gothic Relating to the medieval period,
particularly in architecture, typified by tall
pointed arches, flying buttresses and
elaborate decoration. During the Renaissance
it was seen as a derogatory categorization,
equated with barbarianism. By the mid-
eighteenth century, however, there was a
revival of interest that would continue to
influence contemporary architecture and
design up until the early twentieth century.

grisaille A painting comprised solely of
shades of grey, often mimicking the
appearance of a stone carving.

High Renaissance Period covering the four
decades leading up to the sacking of Rome in
1527, generally considered to have witnessed
the creation of some of the most remarkable
works in the history of western art, including
those by Michelangelo, Raphael and da Vinci.

illuminated manuscript A medieval, or later, manuscript with text adorned by decorations and illustrations in bold colours. The name derives from the common usage of gold highlights within these designs.

medieval Related to the Middle Ages.

monogram Interwoven letters, usually a person's initials, designed to be a motif or logo.

mythology A body of stories, usually containing fictional or fantastical characters, used to reinforce the collective customs and worldview of a particular culture. Classical mythology and its symbolism has been a major source of inspiration for artists since the Renaissance.

naturalism A desire to create an accurate – rather than stylized or idealized – representation of nature in art.

parapet A wall that borders a sudden drop from a roof or balcony.

self-portrait A depiction of him or herself by an artist, either as a singular subject or part of a larger composition.

triptych A picture, often devotional, consisting of three hinged panels. The two external panels normally close shut to conceal the main central panel.

Venus Pudica Meaning the 'modest Venus', this is a term applied to the many copies of the ancient Greek sculpture 'Aphrodite of Knidos' by the fourth-century BCE sculptor Praxiteles. Although the original is now lost, it was widely copied during the Roman period, and its general pose – a *contrapposto* stance, with the figure attempting to conceal her nudity – has appeared widely in painting and sculpture since the Renaissance.

woodcut A type of printmaking in which a carved block of wood is used to carry the design. The surface of the block is cut along the grain with the design standing proud, to which the ink is applied.

PIETÀ

MICHELANGELO BUONARROTI
(1475–1564)

the 30-second artwork

'… it is indeed a miracle that a formless block of stone should be shaped to a perfection that nature herself is scarcely able to create in the flesh'. These words from Vasari's biography of Michelangelo express the sense of awe the beholder experiences before the artist's early masterpiece. A sculpture of exquisite beauty, created at the age of 23 from marble he selected at the quarries of Carrara, it shows the Virgin holding Christ's body on her lap, her left arm extended, palm turned upwards as though to offer his sacrifice to us, her other hand pressing close to the wound in his side. She gazes down with a restrained and serene expression unusual for scenes of lamentation. The sweetness of her young features contrasts with her monumentality, rendered through the heavy drapery on her bust and legs. Christ abandons the pain of the Passion, his body heavy in Mary's arms, his head thrown back, with scarcely any sign of the violence done to his flesh. His idealized body shows none of the rigidity and resistance of traditional depictions of the *Pietà*. It displays instead the beauty and harmony of Michelangelo's classical nudes. This version of the lamentation theme, originating in Netherlandish art, usually depicts a theatrical and gruesome scene. Michelangelo's rendition is far more subdued, intimate and moving.

Michelangelo signed the work on a band across the Virgin's chest: 'Michelangelus Bonarotus Florentinus Faciebat'.

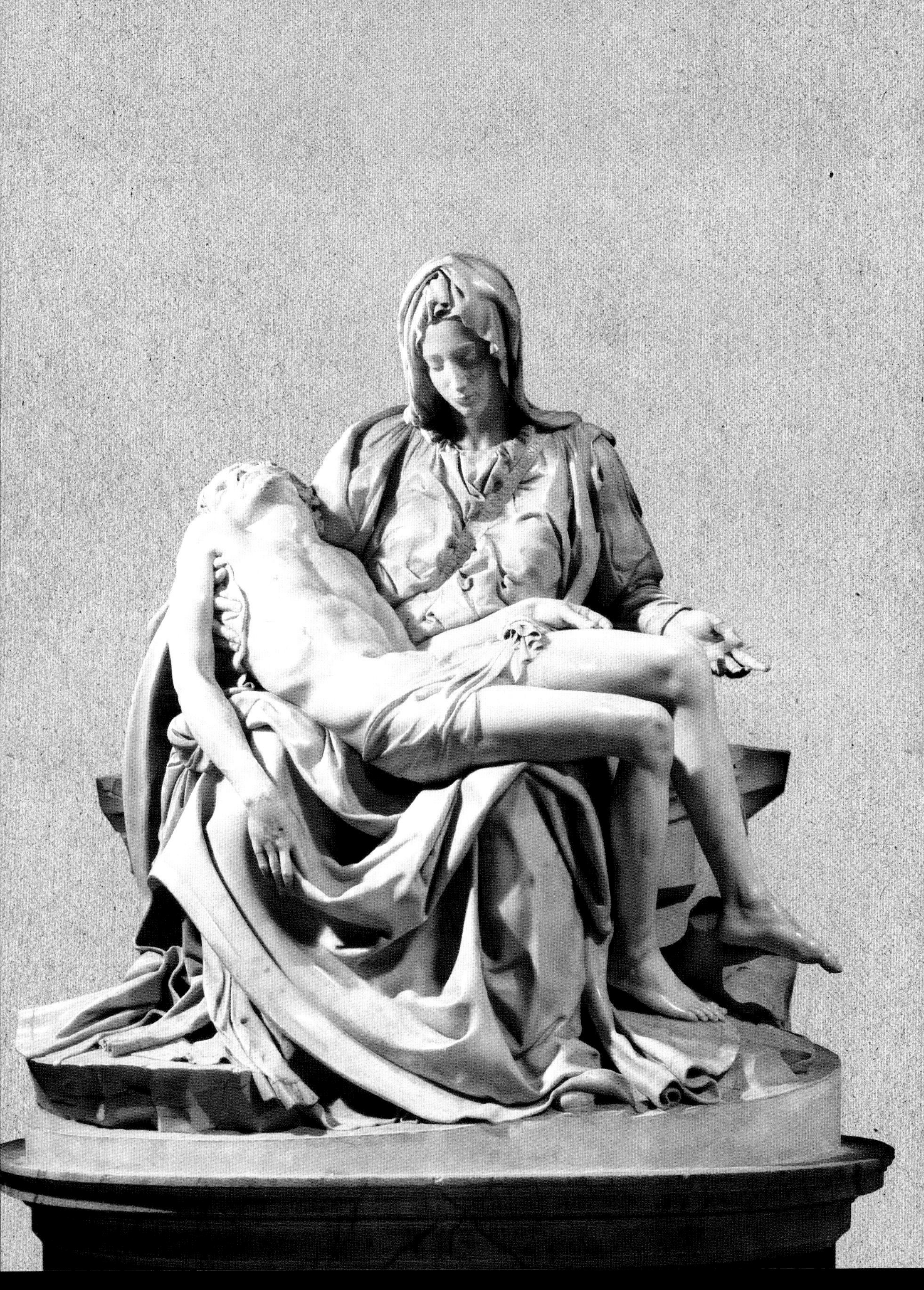

the 30-second artwork

Dürer's drive to improve his art took him in 1494/5 to Northern Italy to study the ideas of the Renaissance. There he was not only influenced by the new style in painting but also by the humanist notion of the artist as a creative individual, rather than just a craftsman. In this painting Dürer faces the viewer head-on with a direct gaze. The composition offers no diversion or distraction from his image: the dark background emphasizes his presence, which fills the entirety of the panel from edge to edge. He has drawn attention to his eyes by framing them with his monogram and an inscription, and to his right hand – his drawing hand – by placing it at the centre of his body. Thus he asserts both his vision and his technical skill as components of his artistic genius. The full-frontal pose is highly unusual in portraiture of this period, when the trend was for a three-quarter view to suggest movement and three-dimensionality. The format Dürer adopts recalls the symmetry and format of devotional images of Christ, known as the Holy Face. It is highly likely that Dürer was deliberately making this allusion. Rather than blasphemy, this has been interpreted as a reference to the artist's creative power. The Latin inscription reads, 'I, Albrecht Dürer of Nuremberg, portrayed myself in appropriate colours, aged 28 years.'

3-SECOND SKETCH
Dürer boldly asserts his status as a celebrated artist, associating himself with the divine image of Christ in this provocative self-portrait.

3-MINUTE STUDY
By 1500 Albrecht Dürer had achieved international recognition as a printmaker, having two years earlier published a series of woodcuts depicting scenes from the Book of the Apocalypse; as a portraitist he was also in great demand from important patrons in his native Germany. In this, his third painted self-portrait, he asserts his own status as a respected artist at the height of his powers.

DETAILS OF THE WORK
Oil on wood panel, 1500
67 x 49 cm (26½ x 19¼ in)
Alte Pinakothek, Munich

3-SECOND BIOGRAPHY
EMPEROR MAXIMILIAN I
1459–1519
Known for extending the power of the Hapsburg dynasty across Europe, using imagery commissioned from Dürer to assert his authority as Holy Roman Emperor, most notably the monumental woodcut *The Triumphal Arch* (1515)

30-SECOND TEXT
Elena Greer

The inscription giving his age is significant: according to medieval thought, 28 marked the transition from youth to maturity.

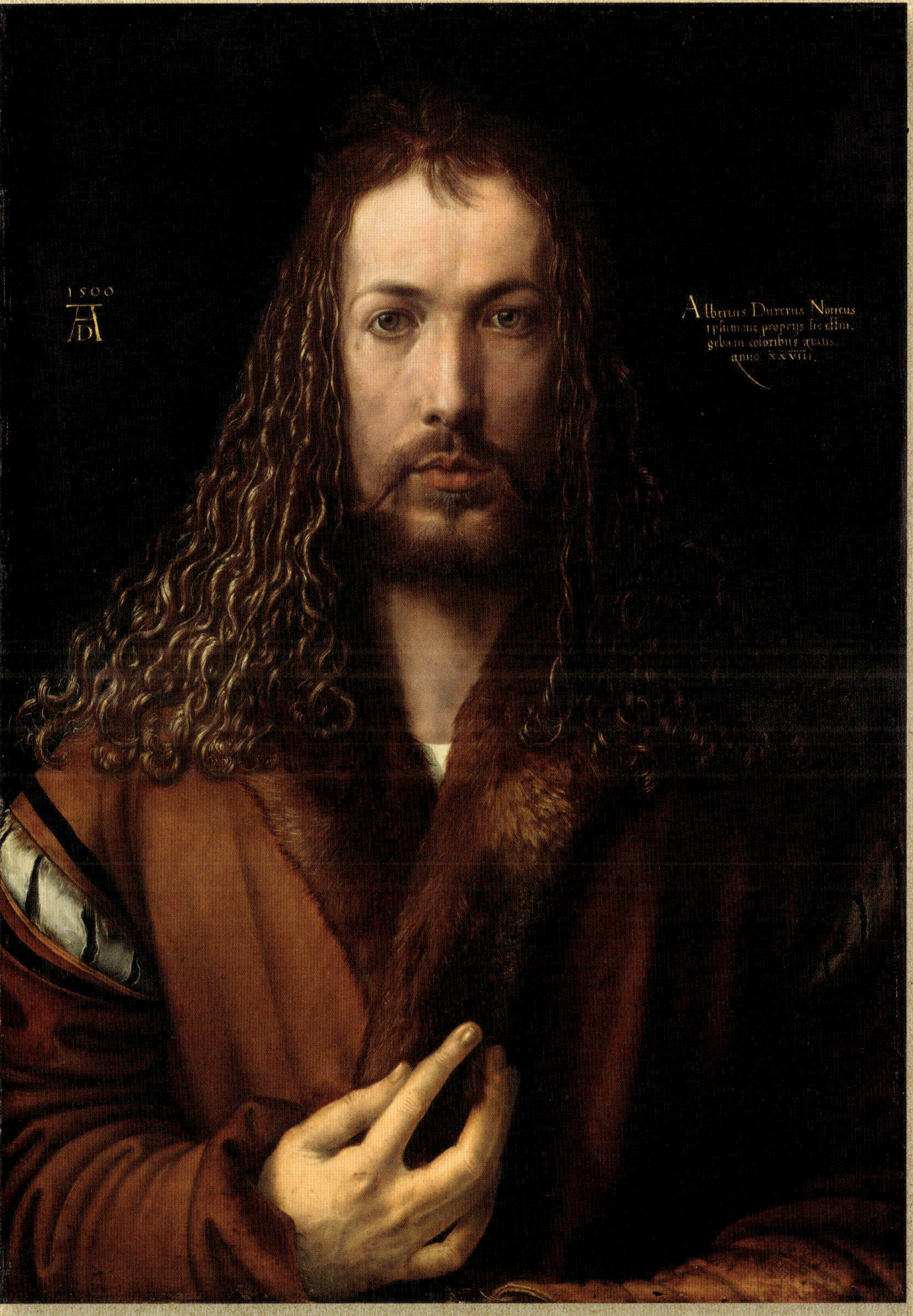

1500
Albertus Durerus Noricus
ipſum me proprijs ſic effin.
gebam coloribus ætatis
anno XXVIII.

the 30-second artwork

Known as the 'strawberry painting' in the seventeenth century, the subject of the main panel of Bosch's triptych has puzzled viewers since it was first displayed. Its current title is a nineteenth-century invention deriving from the sensual pleasures depicted in that panel. Hundreds of naked men and women gorge themselves on ripe fruit, frolic in lakes and engage in amorous activities. Almost every aspect of the depiction is surreal: the berries, like the birds and fish that appear both in and out of the water, are oversized; bears, cattle and other, more fantastical animals are tamed and ridden like horses; a couple embraces in the translucent sphere of a fantastical organic structure that echoes the bizarre vegetal follies in the distance. This scene has been read as an indictment of humankind's lusty sinfulness, especially as the panel immediately to its right is a disturbing vision of hell, where punishments are tailored to individual sins. The panel to its left shows God introducing Eve to Adam in the Garden of Eden – the brief moment before the Fall, referred to here in the figures plucking and eating red apples. This is just one among many plausible interpretations; it is also quite possible that the painting was produced as a conundrum without definitive meaning, for the visual and intellectual stimulation of its courtly patrons.

3-SECOND SKETCH
There have been many interpretations of Bosch's bizarre vision of mankind at play, none of them definitive, but the painting has delighted and intrigued viewers for centuries.

3-MINUTE STUDY
Among the few facts we know about this painting is that it was commissioned by the Count of Nassau, Engelbert II, for his palace at Coudenberg in Brussels. On either side are hinged panels that close over it like cupboard doors; these Bosch painted with a gloomy grisaille image of the earth at the time of its creation, possibly to heighten the dramatic moment when, on opening the panels, this contrasting exotic and colourful scene would be revealed.

DETAILS OF THE WORK
Oil on oak panel, 1490–1500
220 x 195 cm (87 x 77 in)
Museo del Prado, Madrid

3-SECOND BIOGRAPHY
ENGELBERT II OF NASSAU
1451–1504
Descended from an important military family at the Burgundian court, a collector of illuminated manuscripts who commissioned a richly illustrated copy of the *Roman de la Rose*, the medieval text on courtly love

30-SECOND TEXT
Elena Greer

It is the multitude of imaginative and complex vignettes offering seemingly endless new discoveries that make Bosch's Garden playground so compelling.

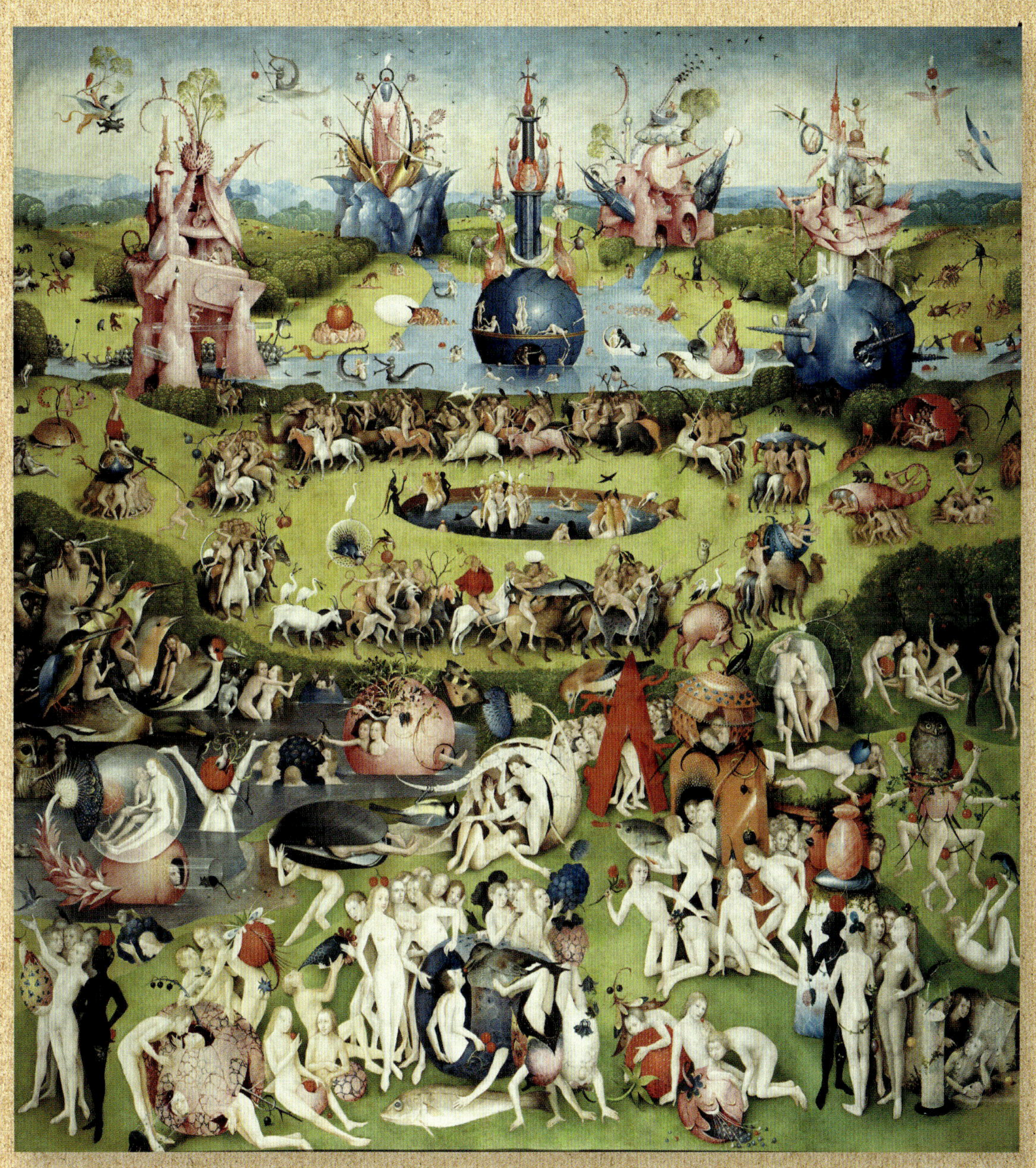

SISTINE MADONNA
RAPHAEL (1483–1520)

the 30-second artwork

Raphael's famous altarpiece was commissioned by Pope Julius II for the church in Piacenza dedicated to St Sixtus, the patron saint of Julius's family. It was located by the main altar, presenting the faithful with a heavenly vision: behind the drawn curtains, the Virgin emerges from a cloud of cherubim, walking towards us and holding the Christ child. Her motion is suggested not only by the gentle *contrapposto* of her feet, but also by the folds of the drapery. Kneeling at her side are St Sixtus and St Barbara, the third-century martyr saint, identifiable by the tower behind her. Leaning on the lower parapet are two *putti*, arguably Raphael's best-known creations. Raphael creates an original rendition of a highly common theme by shedding the earthly sphere and placing the holy group as close as possible to the worshippers. The sense of immediacy is further enhanced by St Sixtus's intermediary gesture, St Barbara's downward gaze and the *puttis'* apparent invasion of our space. The Virgin has the features of Margherita Luti, or *La Fornarina* (the baker's daughter), Raphael's mistress and the subject of two celebrated portraits. St Sixtus recalls Julius II, whose family emblems of oak leaves and acorn decorate the saint's robe and tiara, and St Barbara may be a portrait of Giulia Orsini, Julius II's niece.

3-SECOND SKETCH
While retaining his characteristic harmony, Raphael reinvents a common theme by building a direct relationship between the holy figures and the worshippers standing below.

3-MINUTE STUDY
This altarpiece can be seen as a commemorative picture for Pope Julius II, whose patronage turned Rome into the art capital of Europe. Among his most famous commissions are Michelangelo's Sistine Ceiling, Raphael's Vatican Rooms and the building of the new St Peter's Basilica. The Pope did not live to see the completion of the *Sistine Madonna*, making his likely depiction as St Sixtus and the parapet's allusion to the papal coffin especially poignant.

DETAILS OF THE WORK
Oil on canvas, ca. 1513
265 x 196 cm (104¼ x 77¼ in)
Gemäldegalerie, Dresden

3-SECOND BIOGRAPHIES
ST BARBARA
Died ca.200 CE
Third-century virgin martyr who lived in Asia Minor, imprisoned by her father in a tower and later executed because of her conversion to Christianity

ST SIXTUS
2nd century CE
Pope between 115 and 125, under the Roman emperor Hadrian; his martyrdom is debated

30-SECOND TEXT
Simona Di Nepi

The putti have long been reproduced independently, becoming more famous than the picture itself.

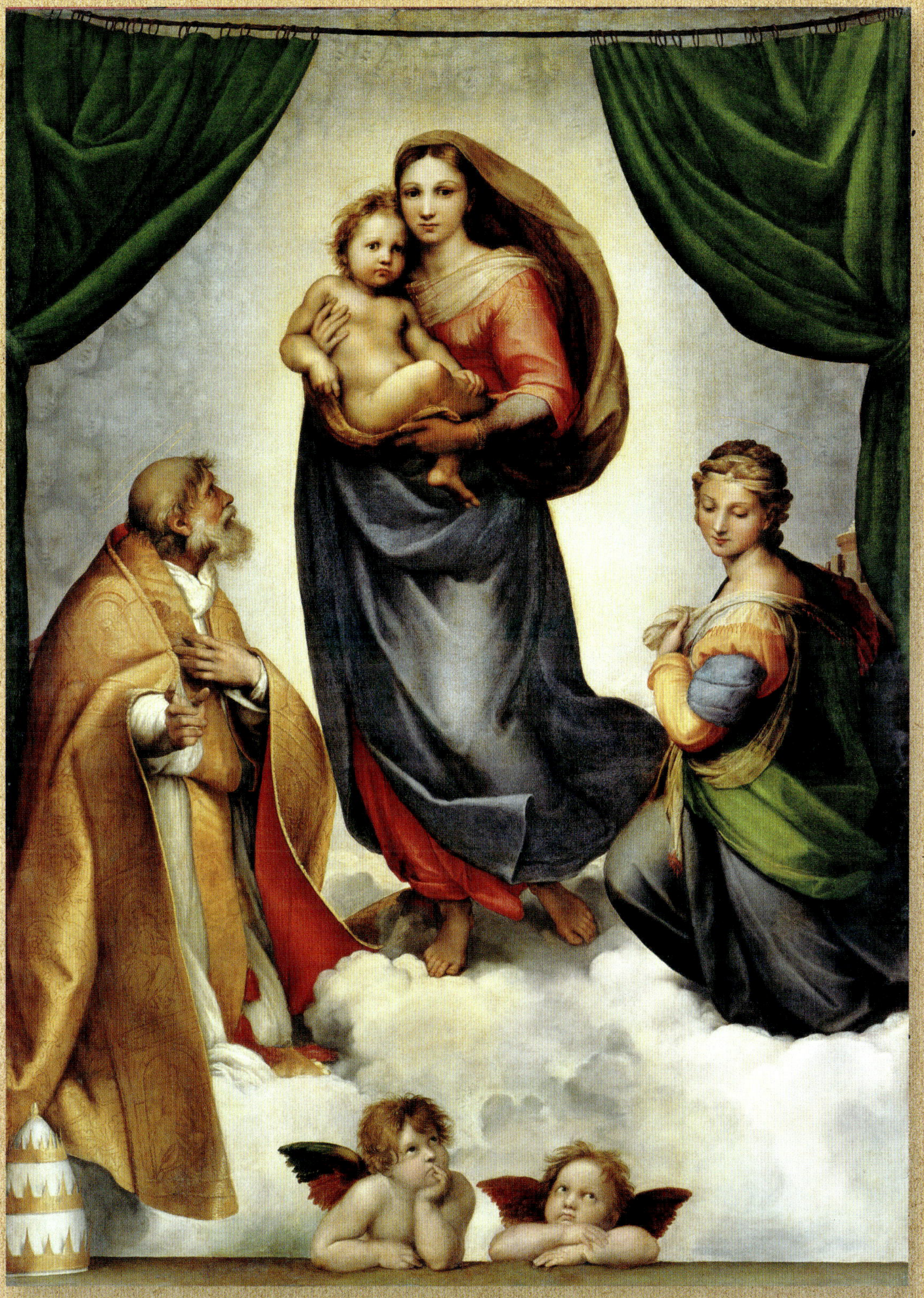

the 30-second artwork

The marble floor of the room in which these two eminent men are standing is decorated with the same pattern as the floor at Westminster Abbey, where in June 1533, the year this was painted, Jean de Dinteville, French Ambassador to England, had attended the coronation of Anne Boleyn, Henry VIII's second wife. Holbein's skill in depicting a range of textures is displayed in the green damask of the curtain, the shimmering pink silk of de Dinteville's tunic and the individually painted knots of the rug that covers the table. The table is arrayed with astronomical, mathematical and musical instruments. On close inspection they reveal discord: the lute has a broken string, the arithmetic book near the globe is open at the page marked 'Divide'. These clues have been interpreted as a commentary on Henry's break with the Roman Catholic Church. If viewed from a particular angle the elongated shape that appears to hover between the men's feet becomes a compact skull. Renaissance portraiture was often commissioned as a reminder of the frailty of life, or memento mori, and therefore the inclusion of skulls was not unusual. Here, in keeping with the rest of the picture, the skull requires deciphering. Equally hidden at the top left of the picture is a crucifix that hints at the hope of redemption in the resurrected Christ.

3-SECOND SKETCH

Holbein portrays the magnificence of these visitors to Henry VIII's court, even while visual clues refer to the strained political and religious climate of the commission.

3-MINUTE STUDY

Holbein painted this double portrait of the French Ambassador, Jean de Dinteville, and his friend, Georges de Selve, Bishop of Lavaur, at the court of Henry VIII. The carefully chosen and meticulously painted objects on the table point to their wealth and their intellectual interests but also reveal the foreigners' attitude to Henry's ongoing power struggle with the papacy.

DETAILS OF THE WORK

Oil on oak panel, 1533
207 x 209.5 cm (81½ x 82½ in)
The National Gallery, London

3-SECOND BIOGRAPHIES

JEAN DE DINTEVILLE
1504–55
One of sixteenth-century France's major art patrons, for whose castle in Polisy this painting was commissioned

GEORGES DE SELVE
ca. 1508-41
Bishop of Lavaur from 1526 and Ambassador in Italy and Germany in the 1530s

30-SECOND TEXT

Elena Greer

Jean de Dinteville holds a dagger case inscribed with his age in Latin: 'aetatis 29'.

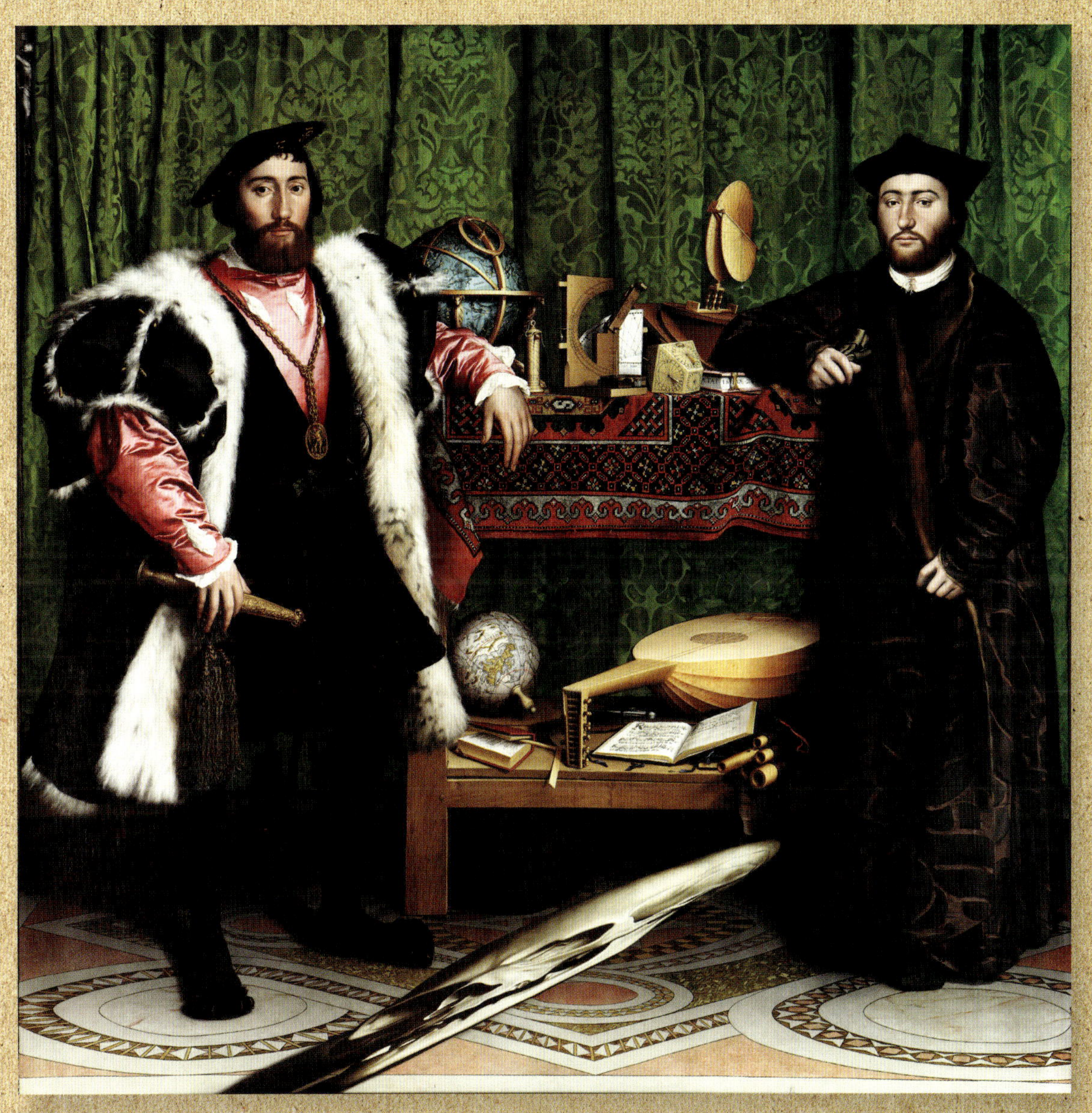

VENUS OF URBINO
TITIAN (1490-1576)

the 30-second artwork

Guidobaldo II della Rovere, the original owner of the painting, referred to the woman in this picture as *la donna nuda*, suggesting that the image portrays a generic idealized beauty in the Venetian tradition of paintings of clothed Renaissance courtesans, known as *belles* (beauties) – usually, like this woman, fair-haired and fair-skinned. By unclothing her and depicting her stretched out, covering – or drawing attention to – her nudity with her left hand, Titian is adapting a picture known as the *Sleeping Venus*, painted by his master, Giorgione, in 1510. Titian's nude is wide awake, however, and confronts the viewer with a gaze of arresting candour. She seems quite aware of her sexuality, holding red roses against her pale skin, which in turn is highlighted by her placement against a deep green curtain. Titian's biographer, Vasari, described the picture as a Venus, but this may be simply because it was so unusual to see a 'real' woman depicted in this way. The setting, too, is decidedly domestic: the women in the background are occupied with a *cassone* – a traditional marriage chest; the spherical myrtle plant also relates to marriage, and the dog is sometimes a symbol of fidelity. The picture may relate to Guidobaldo's own marriage or it may have been painted simply for his private enjoyment.

3-SECOND SKETCH
With this full-length portrait of an archetypal beauty, Titian painted an exquisite example of one of the most popular subjects in art: the nude.

3-MINUTE STUDY
Titian was the leading Venetian painter when he created this arrestingly sexual image of femininity. His mastery of oil paint, which enabled him to build up subtle gradations of colour, perfect for painting flesh and soft fabrics, earned him royal and aristocratic patrons around Europe. As well as portraits, Titian was famous for transforming Classical poetry and mythology into visually enticing images. This picture fits neither category but is simply a celebration of the female nude.

DETAILS OF THE WORK
Oil on canvas, 1538
119 x 165 cm (46¾ x 65 in)
Gallerie degli Uffizi, Florence

3-SECOND BIOGRAPHY
GUIDOBALDO II DELLA ROVERE
1514–74
As Duke of Urbino, one of Titian's most important patrons and a Venetian military commander who fought as a mercenary against the Ottomans in 1559

30-SECOND TEXT
Elena Greer

The woman's pose echoes the **Venus Pudica,** *as in several ancient sculptures of the goddess.*

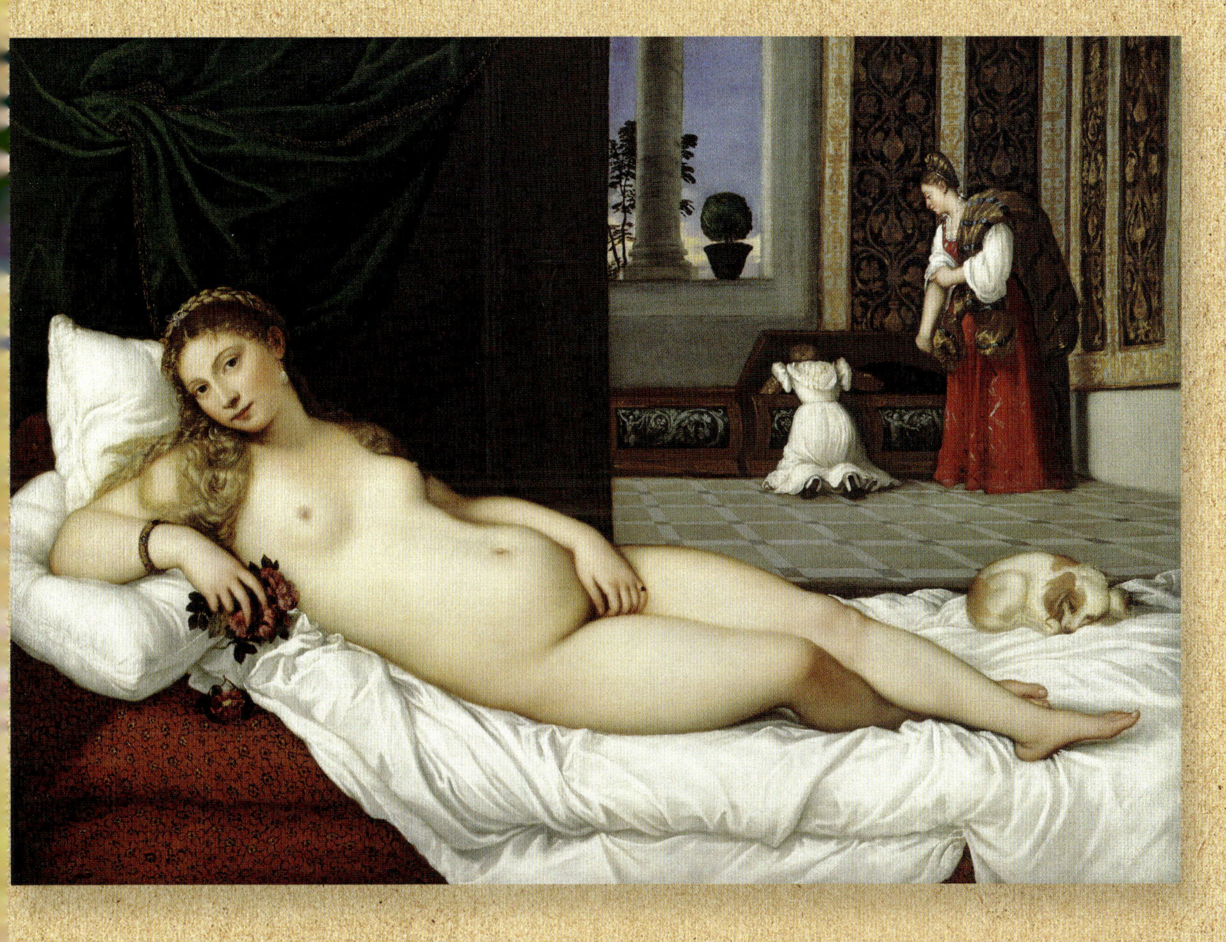

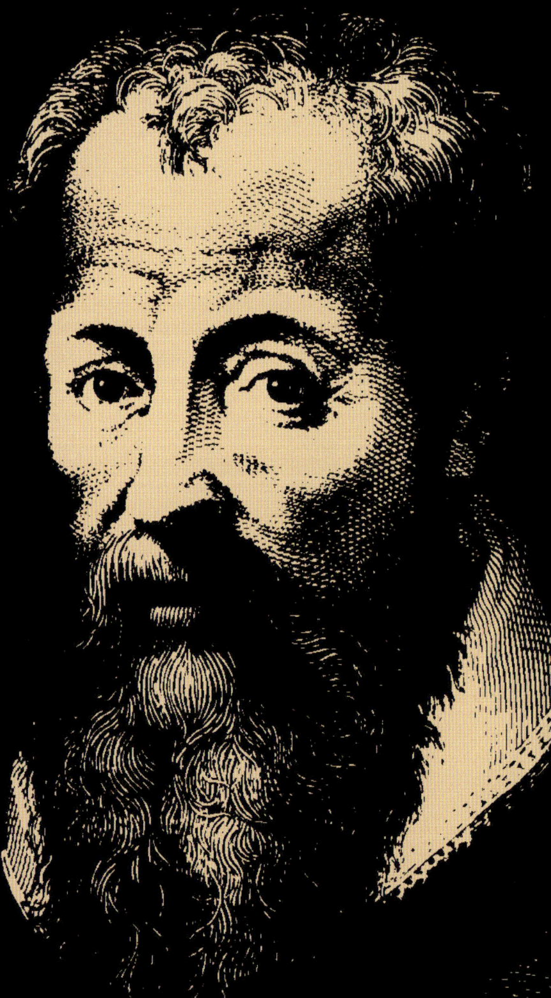

GIORGIO VASARI

Vasari is little known today as a painter although he executed a number of major commissions for important patrons. His main legacy is his three-volume work, *The Lives of the Most Excellent Architects, Painters and Sculptors*, known commonly as the *Lives*. Consisting of anecdotal biographies of Italian artists from the thirteenth to the sixteenth century, the work is the first critical text in the history of art and has influenced the course of the discipline since the publication of the first edition in 1550.

Vasari's early education in Latin, Classical literature and mythology brought him to the attention of Cardinal Silvio Passerini, who, passing through the young boy's hometown of Arezzo in Tuscany and impressed by his learning, persuaded his father to let him come to Florence in 1527. There he trained with a number of notable painters, including Michelangelo, Andrea del Sarto and Baccio Bandinelli.

Vasari had two Medici patrons in the 1530s: Cardinal Ippolito de' Medici and Alessandro de' Medici. After Alessandro's death, he travelled to Rome and Venice before returning to live in Florence in 1554 to work again for the Medici.

His efficiency, speed and ability to organize a large number of assistants meant he was a safe choice for large-scale decorative projects. In the 1550s Vasari's favour with the Medici led to commissions to remodel the Palazzo Vecchio in Florence for Duke Cosimo I and in 1560 to design the Uffizi – now Florence's art gallery, but then offices for the magistrates and civil records – also under the patronage of Cosimo.

According to Vasari, the idea for the creation of the *Lives* came from the scholar Paolo Giovio, who suggested it at a dinner party hosted by Pope Paul III in 1546. The biographies are arranged chronologically and begin with the thirteenth-century painter Cimabue, whom Vasari values, along with Giotto, for his liberation of the art of painting from the 'gothic' style. The colourful anecdotal biographies are a vehicle for Vasari's view of the development of art and reflected the ideas of the Renaissance, *la rinascita* – meaning the rebirth – of art. The extended 1568 edition was a bestseller upon publication, and Vasari's developmental view of art, particularly the significance of the High Renaissance triad of Leonardo, Michelangelo and Raphael, has persisted to this day.

Elena Greer

BAROQUE & BEYOND

allegory An artwork that includes an arrangement of symbolic figures or objects in order to convey a moral, political or philosophical meaning or comment.

antiquarian A person who gains knowledge and understanding of the past through the direct study of ancient objects, artefacts, manuscripts and buildings.

bodegón In Spanish art, a type of still life painting depicting such items as simple vessels, fruit and dead game. Usually set in the everyday austere surroundings of a tavern or kitchen, the still life can be depicted with, or without, human figures.

canon The established basic principles underlying a defined body of artworks, often viewed as the best examples, within art history. In recent decades critics and theorists have questioned the political motivation of traditional canons in western art.

chiaroscuro From Italian, literally meaning 'light-dark', the creation of form in drawing and painting through the subtle gradation and contrast of light and shade, as epitomized by the work of Caravaggio.

courtesan A well educated, cultured and affable female companion to wealthy, upper class, male members of court.

Danse Macabre The 'Dance of Death' is an allegorical subject originating in the late medieval period that symbolizes the inevitability and universality of death. Often depicting a procession, or dance, consisting of representations of death – such as skeletons – leading a range of human characters towards the grave, the theme can also allude to the conceit of earthly possessions and achievements.

genre painting A painting that depicts ordinary scenes from everyday life, albeit often in a sentimental manner. Popular in Dutch art during the seventeenth century, common subjects included taverns, street scenes and domestic interiors.

guild Arising in the medieval period, a formal organization of artists or artisans responsible for standards and training in their particular craft. Based on a hierarchical structure of apprenticeships, journeymen and masters, guilds usually held special privileges regarding the supply of labour within the town in which they were located.

history painting A painting that depicts scenes from the Bible, ancient history or Classical mythology, often on a grand scale. From the seventeenth century onwards it was considered by the European Academies to be the most esteemed form of painting.

humanism A system of beliefs and philosophical thought centred on the importance and influence of humans and their actions, rather than that of divine or supernatural forces.

iconoclasm The destruction of artworks and images on religious, or sometimes, political grounds.

impasto The texture created by paint on a canvas or board. When paint is applied with a greater degree of *impasto*, visible signs of the brushstroke, or other methods of application remain, creating a sense of gestural expression.

mahlstick A long stick that a painter holds in the other hand from the one in which they hold their brush. The padded end of the stick is then rested on the canvas, and the painter is able to steady and support their painting arm along its length.

Mannerist Style in art dating from the sixteenth century characterized by complex and sophisticated compositions. Although influenced by the paintings of the High Renaissance, these later artists tended to reject balance and harmony in favour of asymmetry and exaggerated arrangements of human figures.

scumbling The irregular applications of a thin layer of paint over that of a different colour so the lower level of paint shows through.

studio model A person employed by an artist to undertake different poses from which they can paint, draw or sculpt.

THE CALLING OF SAINT MATTHEW
CARAVAGGIO (1571–1610)

the 30-second artwork

Caravaggio arrived in Rome in 1592, penniless and largely unknown. Within ten years, he had perfected a radically original form of religious painting that provoked praise and consternation from the art establishment of his day. Whereas previous artists had depicted sacred figures as flawless, superhuman beings, Caravaggio turned them into real men and women. Painted from posed studio models, his figures' lifelike gestures and facial expressions seemed to bring the Bible to life. This picture applies his novel approach to the New Testament story of the calling of St Matthew (Matthew 9:9). A tax collector by profession, Matthew had led a life dedicated to amassing personal wealth until Christ invited him to change his ways by becoming one of his apostles. Caravaggio stages the encounter in a gloomy, insalubrious setting, using *chiaroscuro* effects to focus attention on the principal characters in the narrative. Christ's head and summoning hand emerge dramatically from the darkness at far right, suggesting His sudden appearance at the tax collector's place of business. Matthew, whose bearded face is picked out by a shaft of light, points to himself quizzically, unable to believe the call is for him. He still grasps a coin between thumb and forefinger, but his right foot is raised off the ground, indicating his readiness to follow Christ.

A young man seated far left hides a coin in the shadow cast by his hand – an indication of the dishonesty of Matthew's associates.

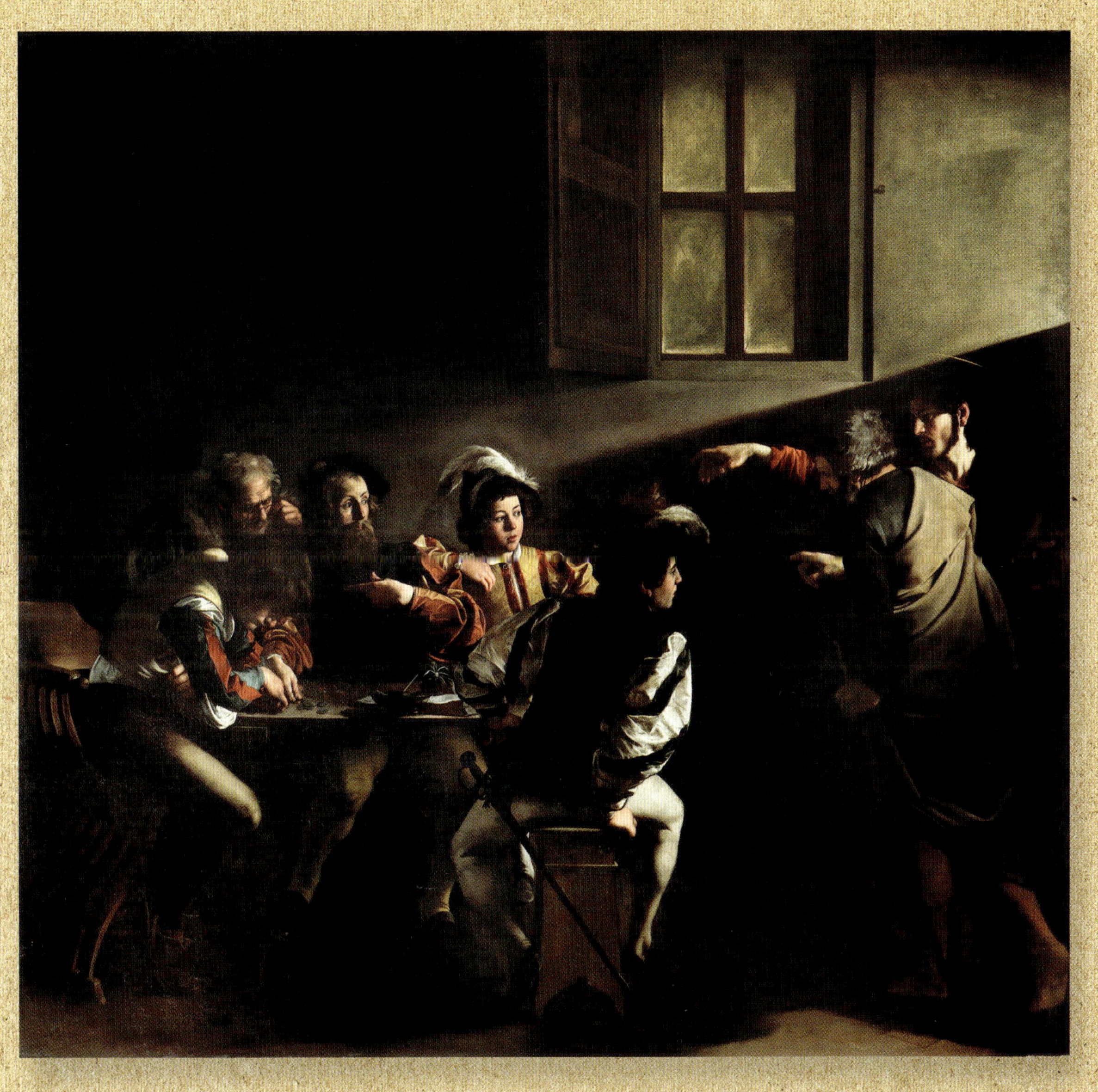

SUSANNA AND THE ELDERS
ARTEMISIA GENTILESCHI (1593–1653)

the 30-second artwork

Born in Rome into a family of artists – her uncle, brother and father Orazio were also painters – Gentileschi was only seventeen when she made this impressive work. Its subject is the Old Testament story of the virtuous Hebrew wife Susanna (Daniel 13). While bathing in her garden, Susanna was spied upon and then accosted by two elders who threatened to accuse her of waiting for a lover if she did not gratify their lust. Having refused them, she was falsely charged and condemned to death, but saved when the elders gave inconsistent testimonies. Male artists often eroticized Susanna by presenting her as a titillating beauty or sexually-willing accomplice. Here, conversely, she shrinks from the elders in revulsion, ducking and twisting in a way that shows Gentileschi's skill in painting the body in motion and in a dramatic *contrapposto* pose. Susanna's foot is still in the water, reminding us that she really had visited the garden to bathe, not to commit adultery. Elevated by the painting's vertical format, the wheedling elders loom over Susanna like a single menacing creature. The man on the left appears to fondle the hair of the other figures, calling to mind the three-way tryst he hopes will shortly unfold.

3-SECOND SKETCH
A leading female artist's interpretation of the story of Susanna, the steadfast wife who was vindicated after rejecting the blackmail attempt of two lecherous elders.

3-MINUTE STUDY
Gentileschi stages the drama in a compact space, free of extraneous detail, and depicts Susanna in a non-idealizing way, with broad hips and a rounded stomach. These strategies recall Caravaggio, an artist who influenced Artemisia and also her father Orazio, who adopted a more realistic painting style after encountering the younger artist's work in the early 1600s. Orazio evidently knew Caravaggio personally: the two artists were jointly sued for libel in 1603.

DETAILS OF THE WORK
Oil on canvas, 1610
170 x 121 cm (67 x 47¾ in)
Schonborn Collection, Pommersfelden

3-SECOND BIOGRAPHY
ORAZIO GENTILESCHI
1563–1639
Artemisia's father supported her career from an early stage, boasting in a 1612 letter that his daughter (then nineteen) was already unrivalled among living artists

30-SECOND TEXT
Thomas Balfe

A skilful handling of a complicated Biblical narrative, this is the earliest known painting to bear Gentileschi's signature.

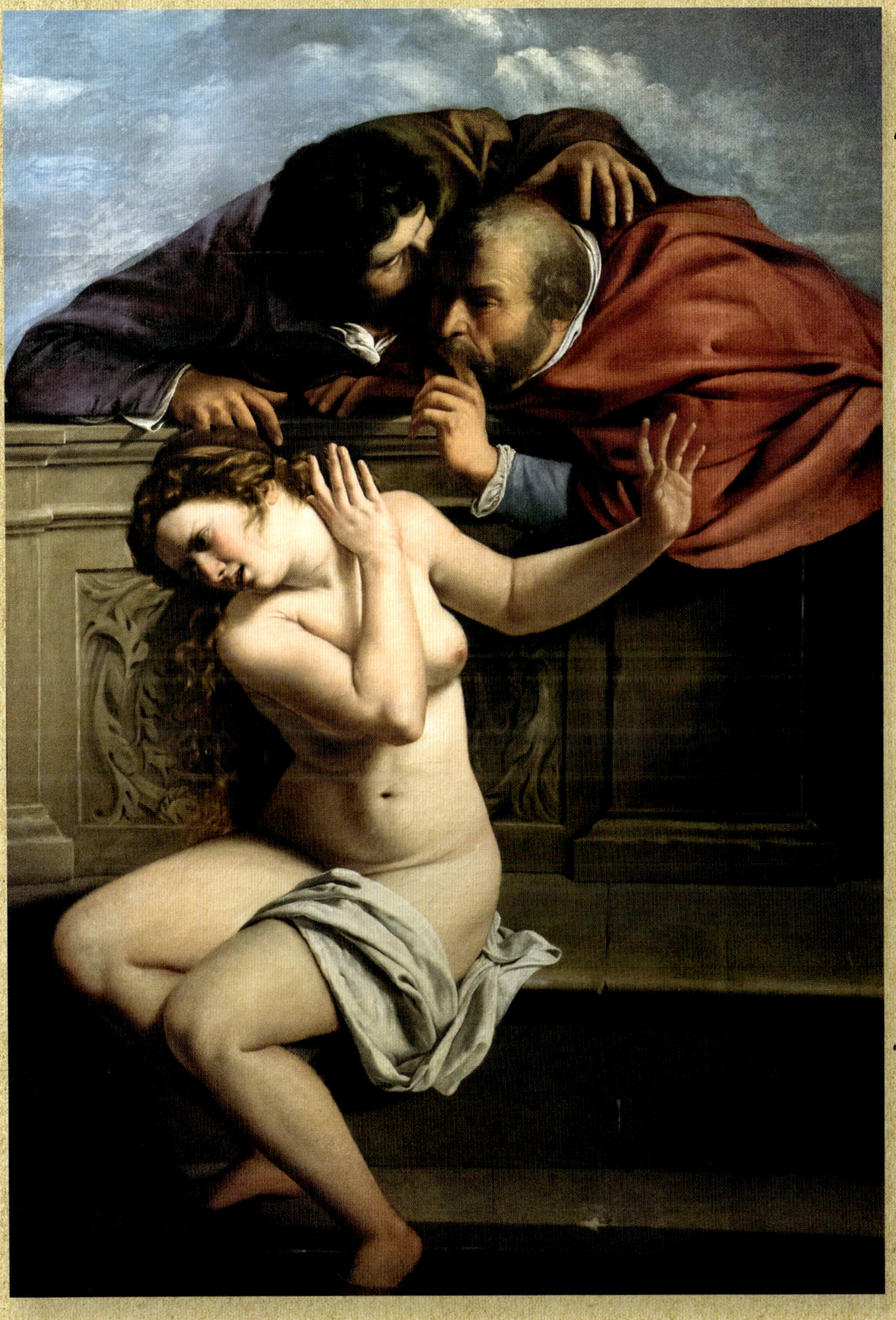

THE LITTLE FUR
PETER PAUL RUBENS (1577–1640)

the 30-second artwork

Peter Paul Rubens was the leading Flemish artist of his generation. Raised a Catholic, he spent much of his early life in Antwerp, studying Latin and modern languages as well as the craft of painting. As a young man he travelled to Italy and was influenced by Classical sculpture and the works of Michelangelo and Titian. Rubens returned to Antwerp in 1608, establishing a studio supplying portraits, history paintings and allegorical and religious imagery to an international clientele. This brought him prosperity and a social position he consolidated in 1630 by marrying Hélène Fourment, daughter of a local merchant, who would bear him five children. In *The Little Fur*, Rubens daringly depicts his wife wearing little more than a short fur wrap. She coyly meets our gaze, her arms encircling her torso in a way that shields, but also draws attention to, her nearly naked body. Her self-protective pose and the fountain behind her evoke Classical statues of the *Venus Pudica* (the love goddess Venus at her bath); her garment references paintings of fur-clad courtesans Rubens would have seen in Venice. If it all seems rather risqué, Hélène's curving abdomen and heavy breasts – those of a nursing mother – remind us that Catholic teaching upheld the legitimacy of sex and childbearing within the divinely sanctioned state of marriage.

Rubens painted his second wife, Hélène, in a pose reminiscent of a bathing Venus.

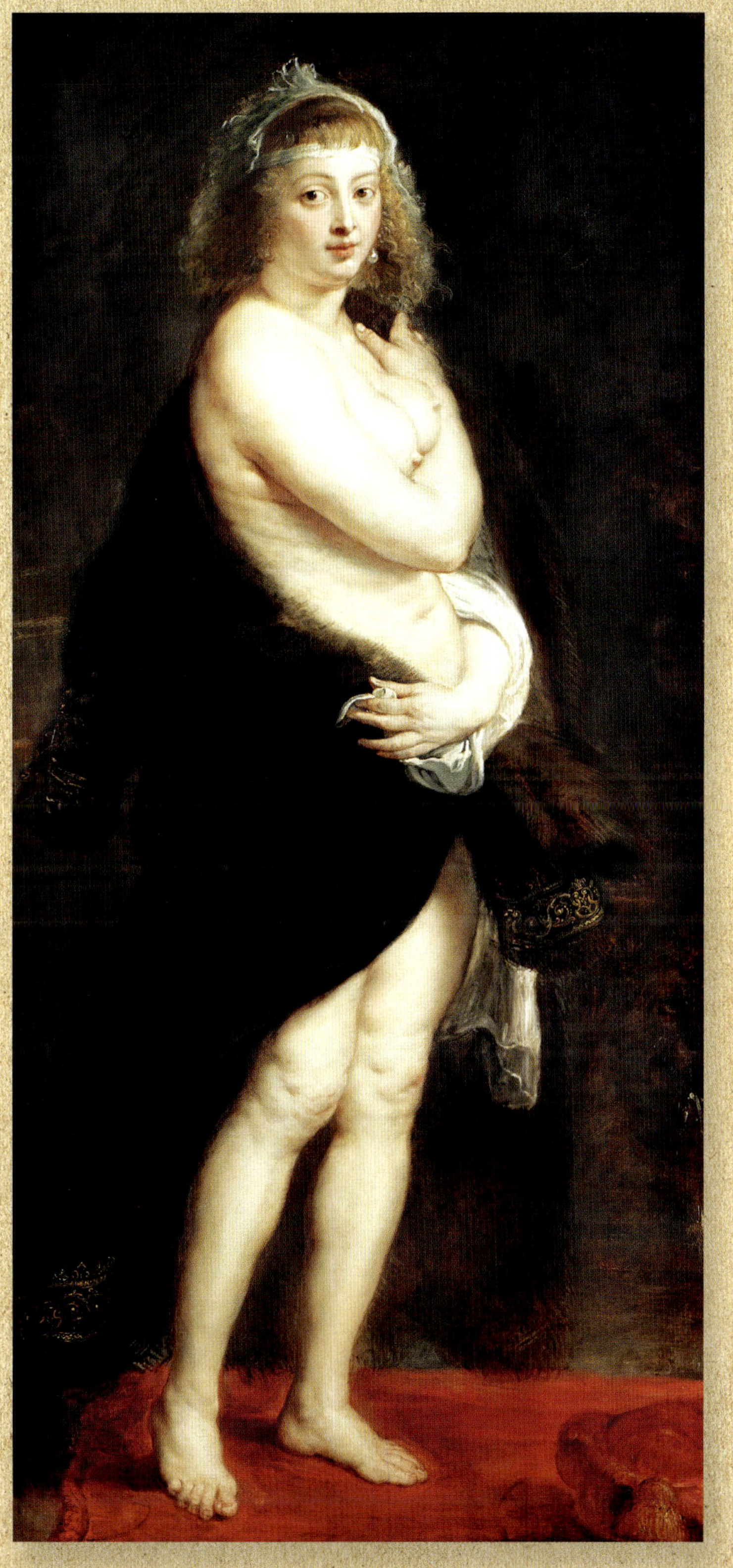

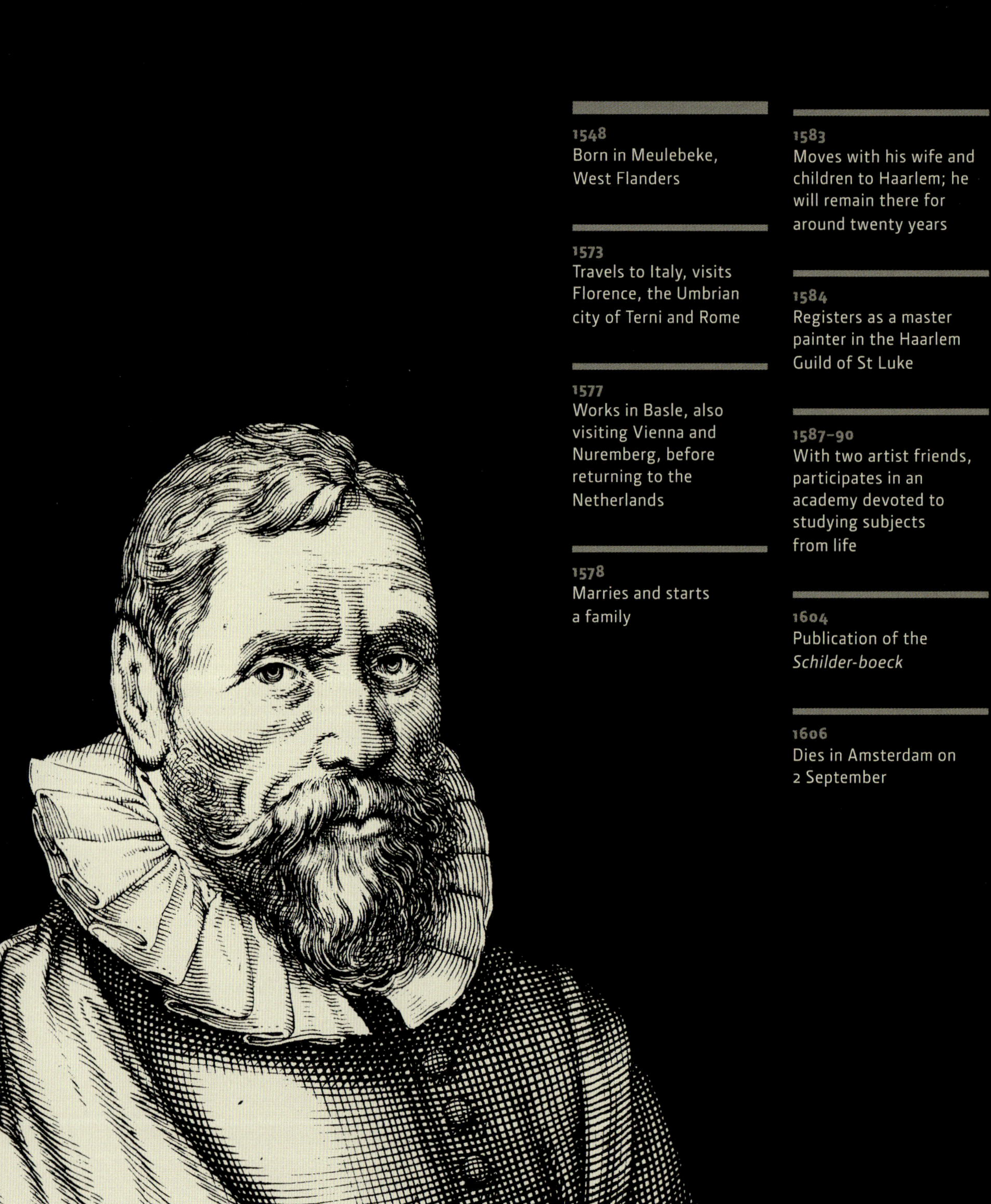

1548
Born in Meulebeke,
West Flanders

1573
Travels to Italy, visits
Florence, the Umbrian
city of Terni and Rome

1577
Works in Basle, also
visiting Vienna and
Nuremberg, before
returning to the
Netherlands

1578
Marries and starts
a family

1583
Moves with his wife and
children to Haarlem; he
will remain there for
around twenty years

1584
Registers as a master
painter in the Haarlem
Guild of St Luke

1587–90
With two artist friends,
participates in an
academy devoted to
studying subjects
from life

1604
Publication of the
Schilder-boeck

1606
Dies in Amsterdam on
2 September

KAREL VAN MANDER

Born in the Flemish town of Meulebeke, Karel van Mander is now best remembered for his *Schilder-boeck* ('Painter-Book'), a major work on art written in Dutch and first published in 1604. A cosmopolitan, well-travelled man, van Mander wrote the book in order to promulgate a new canon of northern European painting – one distinct from, but equal in prestige to, the Renaissance and Mannerist Italian traditions he greatly admired.

The main sections of the *Schilder-boeck* are the *Grondt* ('Groundwork'), a verse treatise offering practical advice to the novice painter, and three sequences of biographies dealing with ancient Greek, Italian and northern European artists. The northern biographies constitute van Mander's enduring legacy; modelled on Vasari's *Vite* (*Lives*), they contain vital information about artists and collectors, as well as descriptions of artworks that were lost to iconoclasm. The *Grondt* is also important. It is one of the most detailed seventeenth-century texts on the practice of painting, and the first to include a chapter on landscape. The remaining biographies are mainly translated from other sources, though the section on Italy does contain some original material – notably, on the work of Caravaggio.

Most of what we know about van Mander himself comes from an anonymous biography published in the second, 1618 edition of the *Schilder-boeck*. His apprenticeship in Ghent to the artist and poet Lucas de Heere prepared the way for his own double career as painter (and prolific engraving designer) and writer – of poetry, plays, works on art, and translations from ancient Greek, Latin, French and Italian. In 1573, travelling to Italy, he encountered Vasari's *Vite* for the first time. He also visited Basle, Vienna and Nuremberg before arriving back in Meulebeke in 1577.

The late 1570s saw an escalation in the violence that had long affected the southern Netherlands as Spain struggled to retain control over the region. In 1583, van Mander and his family moved to Haarlem, a city in the northern Netherlands where their religious views were better tolerated, and where he would remain for most of the rest of his life, working as a painter and producing many important literary works.

Van Mander completed the *Schilder-boeck* in 1604, shortly before his death in 1606. By that time he had moved to Amsterdam, where he died poor but not forgotten: three hundred mourners walked with his coffin to the city's Oude Kerk, where he is now buried.

Thomas Balfe

THE ARCADIAN SHEPHERDS
NICOLAS POUSSIN (1594-1665)

the 30-second artwork

The scion of a minor noble family from Normandy, Poussin is said to have been a studious young man whose education included some Latin. A turning point in his career came in 1624 when he moved from France to Rome, then Europe's leading artistic centre. The city gave him access to the material legacy of the Classical past (statuary, architectural remains, the artefacts of ancient daily life), which he recorded with evident fascination in numerous drawings and sketches. In Rome, he quickly formed an important friendship with Cassiano dal Pozzo, a scholar and antiquarian who introduced him to new ideas and supported him by buying paintings. Poussin's own interests in language, philosophical themes and the Classical past coalesce in *The Arcadian Shepherds*, set in the idyllic land of Arcadia described by the poet Virgil. Accompanied by a beautifully dressed woman, three shepherds contemplate the inscription 'Et in arcadia ego', which is carved into the rural tomb they have just discovered. Interpreters of the painting have long debated whether these are the words of Death, evoking our mortality ('I, Death, am present even here in Arcadia'), or of the deceased, wistfully recalling their time alive ('I, who was once alive, am now dead in Arcadia'). Either way, this sombre work reminds us of the transience of human happiness.

DETAILS OF THE WORK
Oil on canvas, ca. 1637–38
87 x 120 cm (34¼ x 47¼ in)
Musée du Louvre, Paris

3-SECOND BIOGRAPHY
CASSIANO DAL POZZO
1588–1657
Friend of Galileo and a patron of Caravaggio, Artemisia Gentileschi and Gian Lorenzo Bernini, who would eventually acquire around 50 works by Poussin, as part of a vast collection of artworks, curiosities and antiquities

30-SECOND TEXT
Thomas Balfe

The tomb's inscription is partly hidden in shadow so, like the shepherds, we must also decipher the words.

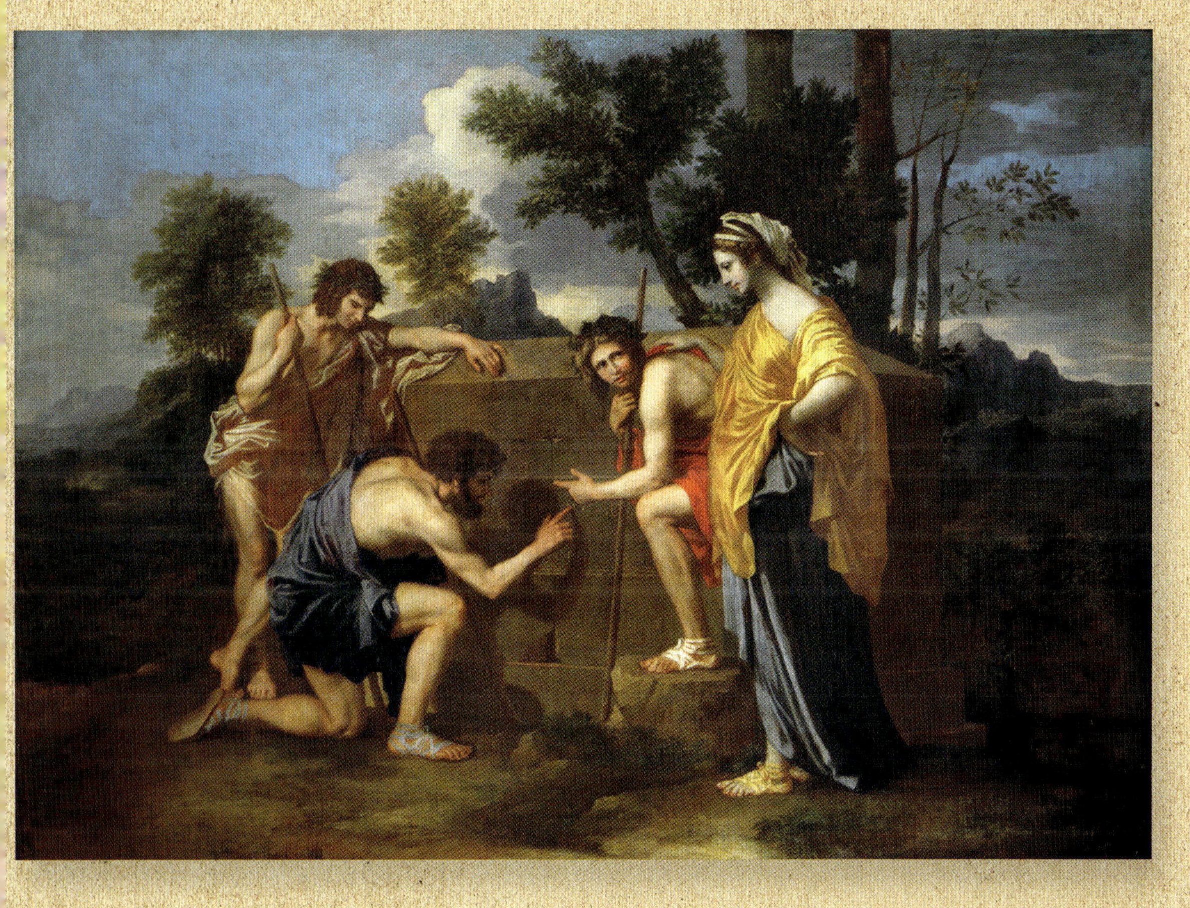

LAS MENINAS
DIEGO VELÁZQUEZ (1599–1660)

the 30-second artwork

Palette, brushes and mahlstick in hand, Velázquez has depicted himself in the act of portraying the Spanish monarchs Philip IV and Queen Mariana. Their reflected forms can just be made out in a mirror hanging at the back of the room where the artist is working. A more prominent presence is the couple's daughter, Margaret Theresa. Resplendent in a wide farthingale dress, the little Infanta is flanked by her maids – the *meninas* of the work's modern title – and attended by two dwarfs, a drowsing dog, a guard and female chaperone, and a chamberlain who watches events from the stairs. By integrating his own image into this intimate depiction of the royal household, Velázquez alludes to his privileged role as court artist. He had gained this position in the early 1620s when, having made his name in Seville as a painter of religious pictures and *bodegones*, he was invited to Madrid and delighted the king with a (now lost) portrait. In this great picture, he also displays his artistic skills at every opportunity. The rendering of the mirror's gleam with scumbling, the play of window light, and the use of flecked white highlights to capture the sheen of dress silk all showcase his ability to turn oil paint into a cunning reflection of reality.

The reflection in the mirror shows either the royal couple or the portrait Velázquez is painting.

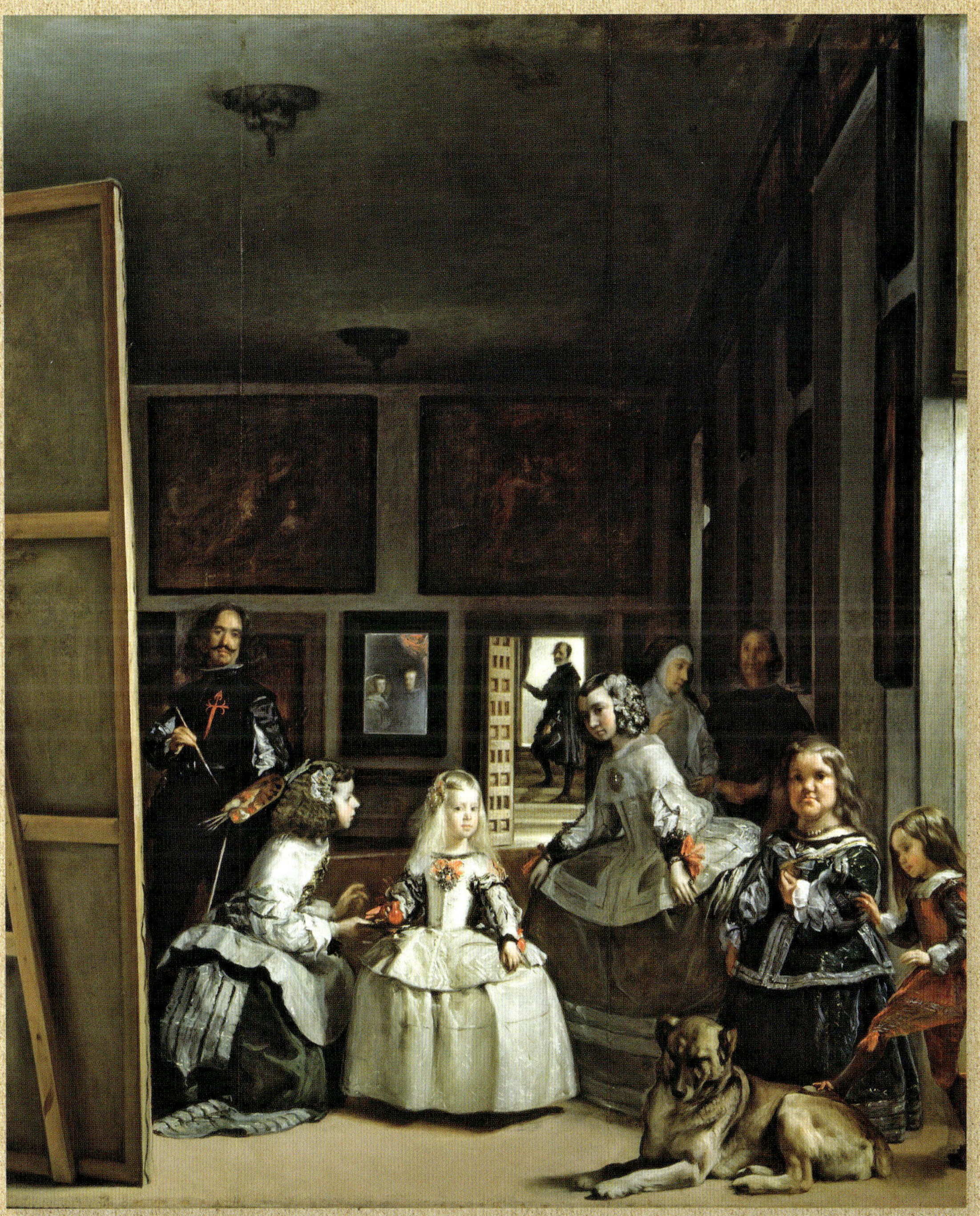

THE MILKMAID
JOHANNES VERMEER (1632–75)

the 30-second artwork

The work's modern title

notwithstanding, the woman Vermeer has depicted here is a kitchen maid. Standing before a bare wall whose every stain and hollow has been painstakingly described, she is shown making pudding, or perhaps porridge, from the bread on the table and the milk she is pouring into a redware bowl. In Dutch genre paintings of the period, kitchen maids are routinely associated with laziness and lust. They often carry a pot, pan or jug, signifying their empty-headedness or willingness to be a receptacle for male desire. Vermeer decisively reverses this cliché. His use of a low viewpoint turns the maid into a dignified, even imposing figure. The painting's midpoint coincides with the core of her sturdy, columnar body, suggesting her pivotal role in supporting the household. Vermeer worked as an art dealer as well as an artist and was only about twenty-five when he completed this work. Its first viewers, probably including the artist's main patron, Pieter van Ruijven, would have enjoyed not only its upending of genre-painting conventions but also how different textures have been captured with an astonishing variety of brushstrokes and pointillés – a patchwork of touches resolving into perfect visual order when the work is seen from an appropriate distance.

The basket, bread and vessels on the table all show Vermeer's characteristic use of pointillés.

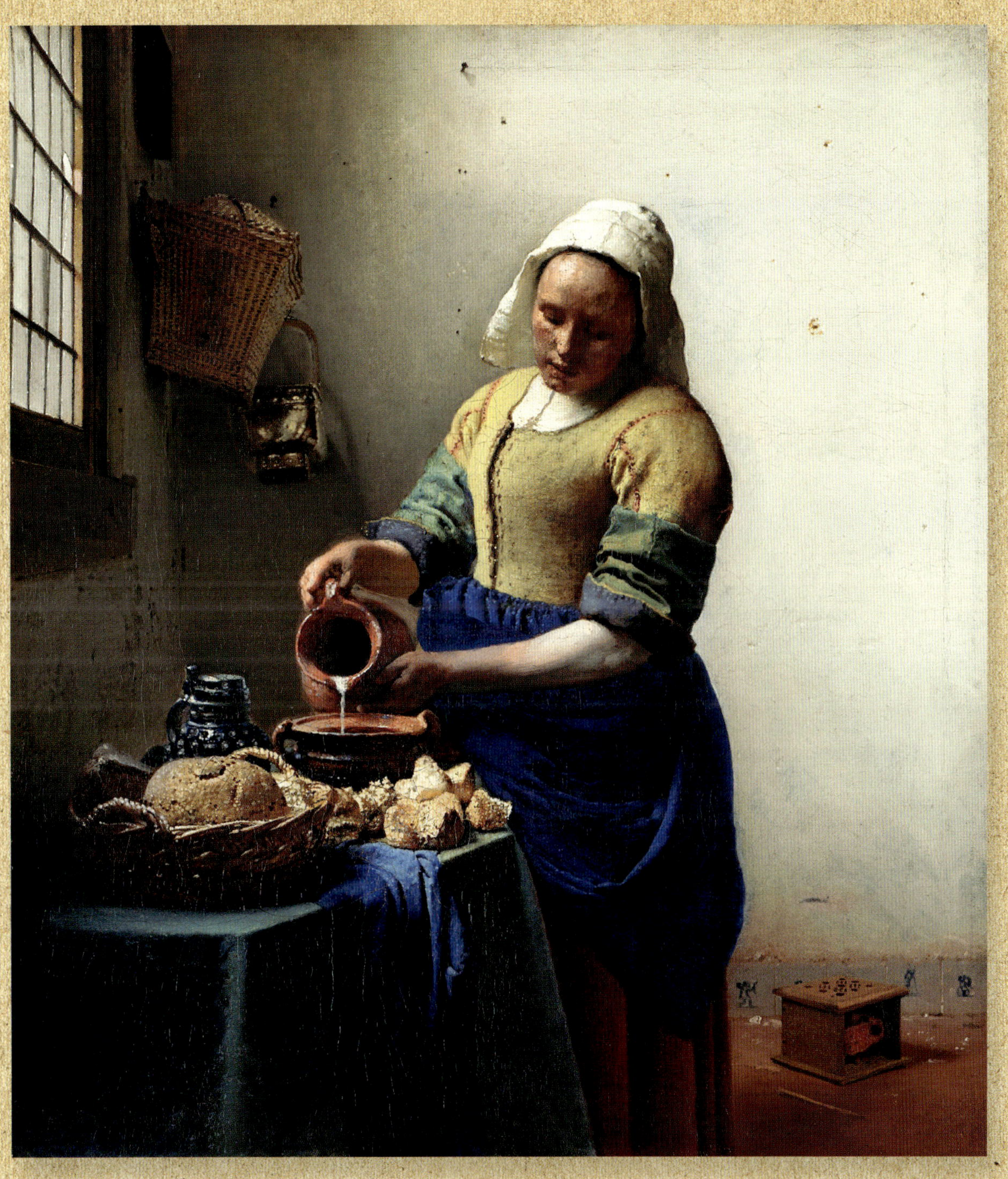

SELF-PORTRAIT
REMBRANDT VAN RIJN (1606–69)

the 30-second artwork

The years leading up to this

self-portrait were a troubled time for Rembrandt. In the mid-1650s, the middle-aged Dutch artist was forced to declare himself insolvent and to auction off many of his cherished prints and drawings. It was a significant reversal for someone who as a younger man had been known for his lavish spending. Rembrandt's career had taken off in 1631 when he moved from his native Leiden to Amsterdam. There, local art dealer Hendrick van Uylenburgh helped him to establish himself. By the early 1640s he was one of the city's leading artists, his face and name known internationally from his many painted and etched self-portraits. Rembrandt used self-portraiture not only to spread his fame but also to control his public image. This painting flaunts his ability to handle thick *impasto* with confident, improvisatory strokes, as in the curls of hair around the left ear, scribbled with the brush handle into still-wet paint. The opulent beret with its gold band declares a level of wealth that he in fact no longer enjoyed, and also recalls Raphael's famous portrait of Baldassare Castiglione, the humanist renowned for his learning and courtly sophistication. Personal problems notwithstanding, here Rembrandt celebrates himself as skilled painter, cultured man and worldly success all at once.

3-SECOND SKETCH
Painting himself at 53, Rembrandt asserts his worldly success and displays his ability to transform thick, loosely handled paint into a convincing portrait likeness.

3-MINUTE STUDY
The eighty or so self-portraits that Rembrandt produced are not simply a record of his changing appearance. He also used the genre to practise depicting facial expressions and different social types. His self-portraits show him grimacing, weeping and laughing, or playing the role of courtier, beggar, madman, sultan, painter and even scimitar-wielding Turkish warrior.

DETAILS OF THE WORK
Oil on canvas, 1659
84.5 x 66 cm (33¼ x 26 in)
National Gallery of Art, Washington

3-SECOND BIOGRAPHY
HENDRICK VAN UYLENBURGH
ca. 1587–1661
Lodged Rembrandt at his house in the early 1630s, securing portrait commissions and paying pupils for him, with the painter marrying the art dealer's niece, Saskia, in 1634

30-SECOND TEXT
Thomas Balfe

The sketchy rendering of the artist's hands draws attention to his weathered face and melancholy expression.

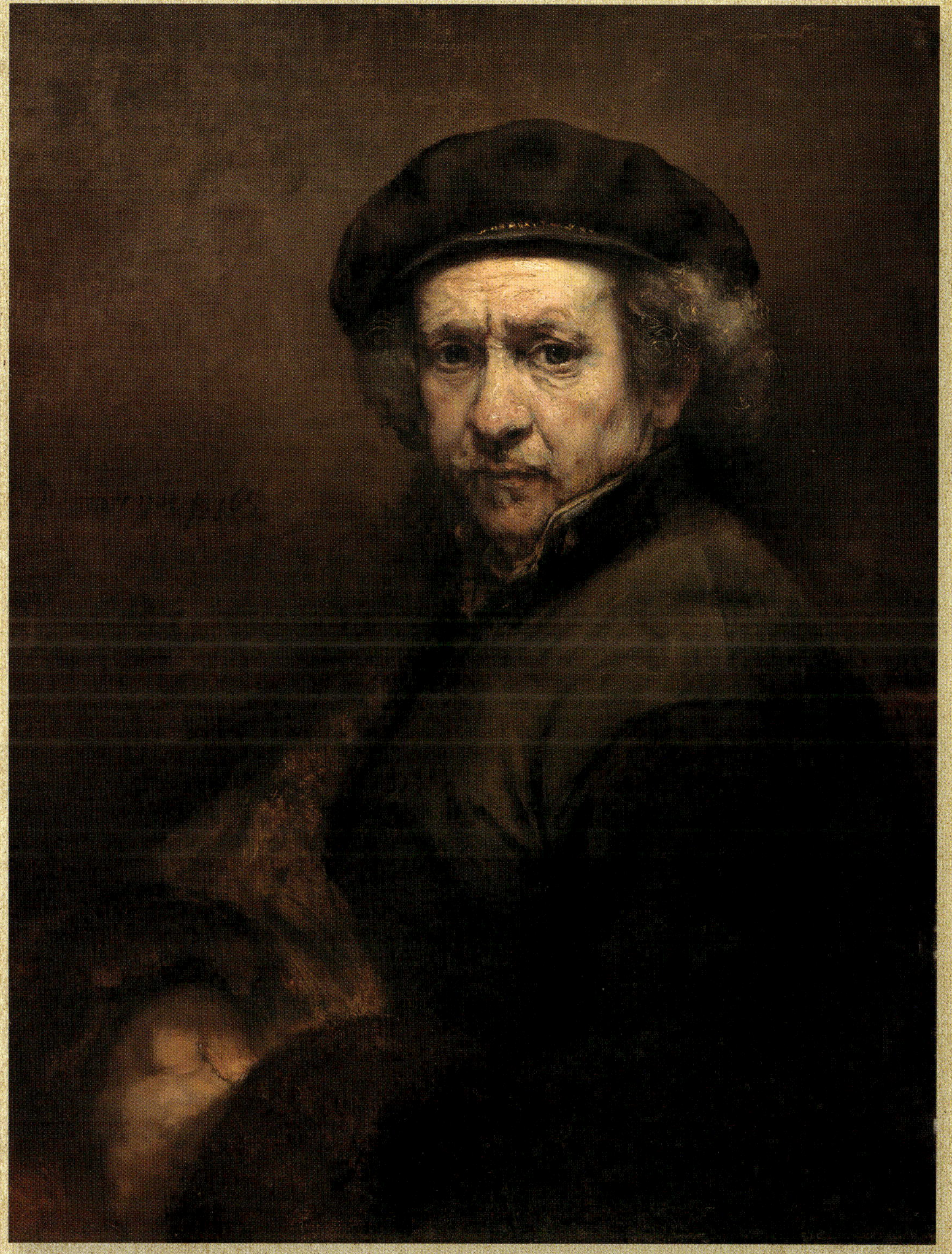

NEOCLASSICISM & ROMANTICISM

Académie des Beaux-Arts Academy of Fine Arts founded in Paris in 1816 to unify the three previously distinct academies of painting and sculpture, music, and architecture established in the seventeenth century.

composition The arrangement and combination of elements within a painting or sculpture that creates the overall appearance of the artwork.

cosmopolitan Consisting of people and influences from many different countries and cultures.

foreground In a painting, drawing or photograph, the area of a depicted scene that appears to be nearest to the viewer.

foreshortening The use of perspective to create the illusion that an object or person, when positioned at an angle to the picture plane or disappearing into the distance, is longer than it has actually been depicted.

gaze The act of looking or being looked at. In late twentieth-century critical theory, the gaze has been considered in terms of power and control, in particular the notion that in the history of western art the gaze is predominately male, with the female subject its recipient.

Grand Tour Educational and cultural tour of Europe popular from the seventeenth to the early nineteenth century undertaken by the wealthy, in particular young men. An essential part of the tour was cultivation in the Classical and Renaissance heritage of Italy, resulting in a fashion for Neoclassicism across Europe.

iconography An artwork's image or content, for example, its subject matter or symbolism, as distinct from its style.

in the round A sculpture conceived and made to be viewed from all sides, or the act of viewing an artwork in this way.

landscape A painting or drawing in which a view of the natural world is the prime focus. Although partial, often stylized landscapes were a common element in the background of religious paintings throughout the Renaissance, it only became recognized as an important subject for art in its own right during the seventeenth and eighteenth centuries.

modernity Relating to the post-medieval, modern period. In art terms it is recognizable in a range of attitudes and conditions, including a rejection of tradition, a desire to convey the contemporary moment, its technologies and cultural mood, a commitment to progress and change, and individual liberty.

nude The depiction of a naked human body in art, often as an expression of ideal beauty and taste. In part due to its status in Classical and Renaissance periods, it became one of the most established and revisited genres in western art.

picturesque Originating in writings of the late eighteenth century, a type of landscape viewed as idyllic and inspiring for artists. In painting, the picturesque landscape will often juxtapose the irregular aspects of nature with signs of a human presence, such as the stone ruins of a castle or a quaint cottage.

plaster Also known as 'plaster of Paris', a fine white powder that, when mixed with water, sets solid. A common material used by sculptors, it can be poured into a mold to form a cast, or applied in layers to a structure, often made of wire mesh.

Romanticism Movement in art and literature arising in the late eighteenth century that favoured subjectivism, and the expression or evocation of emotions and feelings. In painting, it was closely associated with the rising popularity and development of the landscape genre and the wider celebration of nature. It is usually viewed as a rejection of the ordered balance and rationality of Classicism.

staffage Small human or animal figures used within a composition to add interest to a landscape or architectural scene. These figures act as accessories rather than being the primary subject of the artwork.

sublime A categorization of landscape that gained popularity during the eighteenth century. It was based on the principle that imposing natural views can create a sensation of awe, wonderment and sometimes terror in the mind of the beholder.

topographical Relating to the placement or representation of the physical characteristics of a landscape or built environment.

VENICE: THE BACINO DI SAN MARCO FROM THE CANALE DELLA GIUDECCA
CANALETTO (1697–1768)

the 30-second artwork

This painting is one of a pair of *vedute*, or views, depicting Venice's waterfront by the Venetian-born artist, Canaletto. Centred on the bustling waterways of the main island's quayside, it places the viewer right in the middle of the canal's busy hum. Up ahead, at the tip of the island of Giudecca, lies the church of San Giorgio Maggiore, while on the quayside to our left stands the globe-topped Dogana da Mar, Venice's custom house. Canaletto altered the size of the Dogana, making it appear much smaller than it does in reality, so that he could squeeze in the Library next door. Playing with topographical accuracy became one of Canaletto's most frequently employed artistic strategies. By representing multiple landmarks in one composition, he could increase the likelihood of his pictures selling amongst Venice's wealthy tourist clientele. Detailed observation of everyday life was another hallmark of Canaletto's work. His attention to the different costumes and actions of his figures established them as individuals as opposed to mere staffage. Likewise, his depiction of the shipping is highly varied, showing the rich assortment of daily business taking place in eighteenth-century Venice, then one of the world's greatest trading powers.

3-SECOND SKETCH
Canaletto presents a cosmopolitan view of Venice's waterfront, the Bacino di San Marco, with all the hallmarks designed to appeal to tourist-buyers: famous buildings, shipping, animated figures and a bright palette.

3-MINUTE STUDY
By the eighteenth century, Venice was one of the world's leading tourist destinations, exercising a magnetic hold on the imagination of young, wealthy gentlemen undertaking the Grand Tour. The Grand Tourists' purchase of continental artworks became widespread. Back home, these works transformed the appearance of country houses and became powerful signifiers of their owners' knowledge and taste acquired abroad.

DETAILS OF THE WORK
Oil on canvas, ca. 1735-44
130.2 x 190.8 cm (51¼ x 75 in)
The Wallace Collection, London

3-SECOND BIOGRAPHY
FRANCIS SEYMOUR-CONWAY, 1ST MARQUESS OF HERTFORD 1718–94
British politician who acquired this painting and its pair, showing the Bacino di San Marco from San Giorgio Maggiore (also in the Wallace Collection), most likely as a memento of the Grand Tour he made in 1738–9

30-SECOND TEXT
Sarah Moulden

Canaletto presents an attractive, clearly identifiable view of bustling commercial life on a Venetian canal.

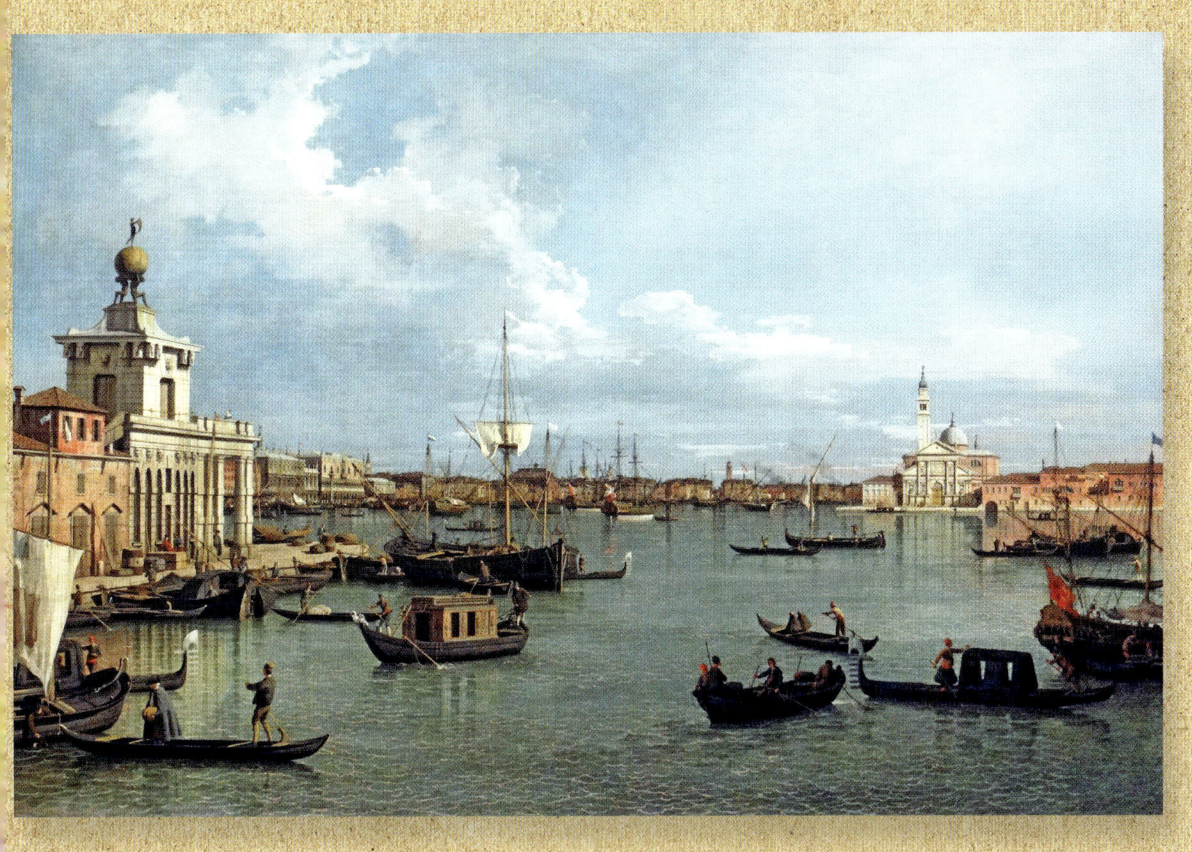

MRS ABINGTON AS MISS PRUE IN LOVE FOR LOVE BY WILLIAM CONGREVE

SIR JOSHUA REYNOLDS (1723–92)

the 30-second artwork

By the early eighteenth century, the theatre in Britain was thriving, with women performers playing a central role in the creation of a spectacular celebrity culture. The rise of the actress went hand in hand with the popularity of the actress portrait, a form of portraiture representing female stars either on or off stage. Reynolds's half-length of Frances Abington, one of the most celebrated performers of the day, is a remarkable example of this new subgenre. It shows an intimate portrayal of the actress wearing fashionable attire and leaning suggestively over a Hepplewhite chair back. Abington is shown in one of her most successful roles, the young and innocent Miss Prue from William Congreve's 1694 comedy *Love for Love*, then enjoying a revival on the London stage. In the play, Miss Prue is a 'silly awkward country girl' who, to the eighteenth-century theatregoer, would have seemed coquettish, even sexually transgressive. The (overly) flirtatious associations of Abington's stage role are reinforced in this portrait by her provocative pose. Reynolds offers us a close-up and level view of Abington, who boldly returns our gaze as she coyly brushes her thumb past her partially opened lips, a gesture that would have been regarded as unusually direct and indecorous for a lady.

DETAILS OF THE WORK
Oil on canvas, 1771
76.8 x 63.8 cm (30¼ x 25⅛ in)
Yale Center for British Art, New Haven, Connecticut

3-SECOND BIOGRAPHY
FRANCES ABINGTON
1737–1815
Celebrated member of David Garrick's company at the Theatre Royal, Drury Lane, with a complex personal life and a reputation as a leading woman of fashion

30-SECOND TEXT
Sarah Moulden

One of at least six portraits of the actress Mrs Abington painted by Reynolds, this half-length is believed to have been painted for a private client.

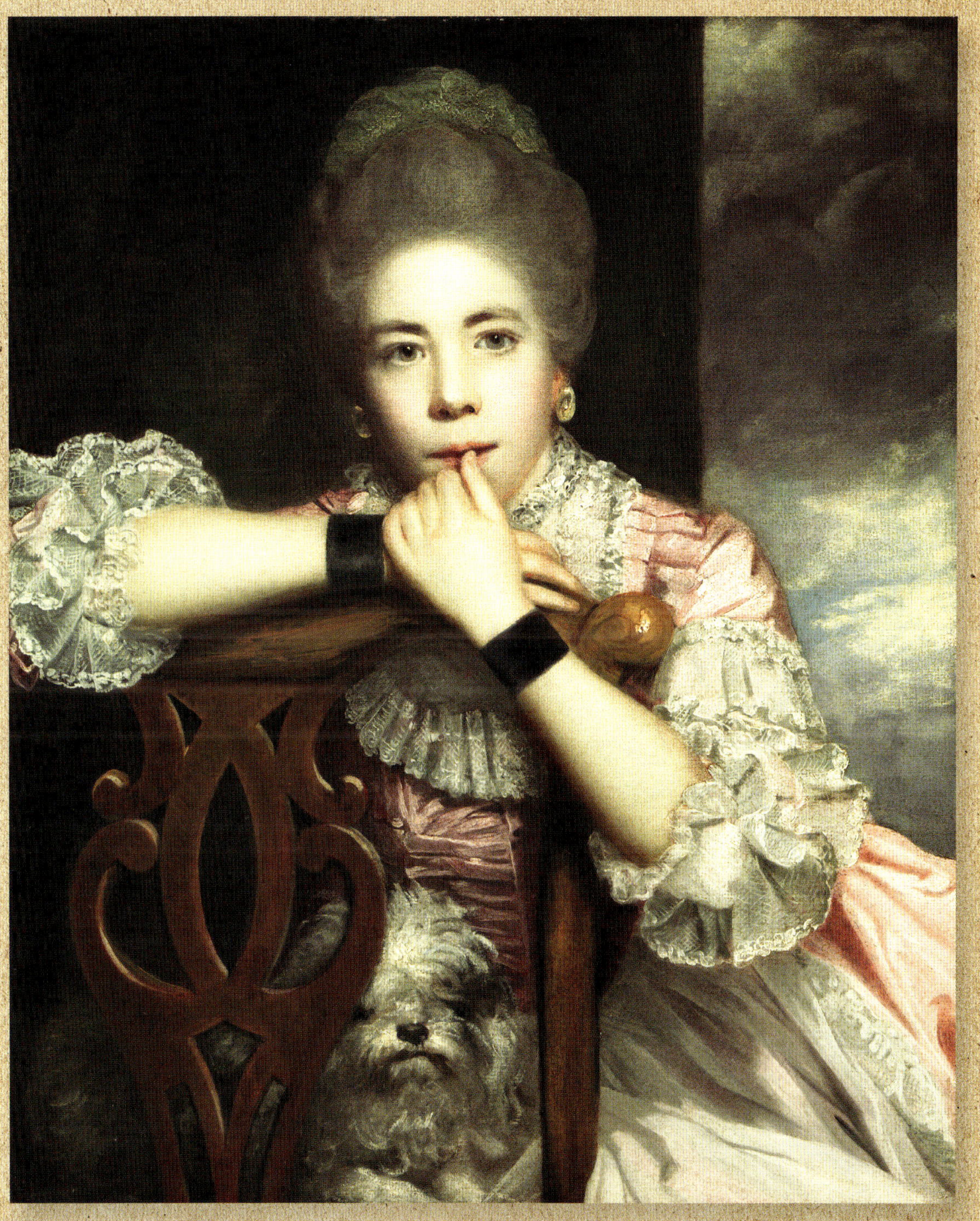

the 30-second artwork

The legend of Cupid and Psyche

was a common subject in eighteenth-century artistic practice. In this life-size marble sculpture, the Italian artist Antonio Canova shows the young lovers in a passionate embrace, Cupid caressing Psyche's face with his right hand while his left covers her right breast. She descends into Cupid's hold, taking his head between her hands and pulling his face closer to hers in an intense interchange of gazes. This is the moment after the winged God of Love has kissed his lover to revive her from a deep sleep induced by inhaling hazardous fumes brought up from the Underworld. The narrative drama is heightened by Canova's use of a dynamic composition. Sharp diagonals, such as Cupid's wings and flexed leg, give the sculpture an upward thrust, while serpentine forms, such as Psyche's languishing torso, anchor it solidly to the rock upon which she lies. This combination of horizontal and vertical accents lends great movement to the work, prompting the viewer to examine the sculpture in the round. Indeed, it was designed to be turned on its mobile base using a handle. The sculpture is also striking for its exceptionally high level of finish. The couple's hyper-smooth skin was obtained using a number of fine files, allowing Canova to model the marble with great precision.

3-SECOND SKETCH
Canova made this life-size sculpture at the age of 30. It depicts the moment when Cupid, God of Love, rescues his lover, Psyche, from a death-like sleep.

3-MINUTE STUDY
The making of *Psyche Revived by Cupid's Kiss* involved a number of precise steps. To help decide the exact composition, Canova worked from various preparatory drawings and small *modellos* (models). Next he prepared a full-scale clay *modello* of the finished composition, of which a plaster mould was taken. The mould then created the basis for a plaster cast that corresponded to the composition's final dimensions, which could then be transferred to the block of marble for carving.

DETAILS OF THE WORK
Marble, 1787
155 x 168 cm (61 x 66¼ in)
Musée du Louvre, Paris

3-SECOND BIOGRAPHY
SIR JOHN CAMPBELL
1753–1821
Scottish army colonel who met Canova in Naples in 1787 and commissioned this sculpture, along with another one of Cupid and Psyche standing

30-SECOND TEXT
Sarah Moulden

This dramatic sculpture is among the most iconic images of sexual love in Western art.

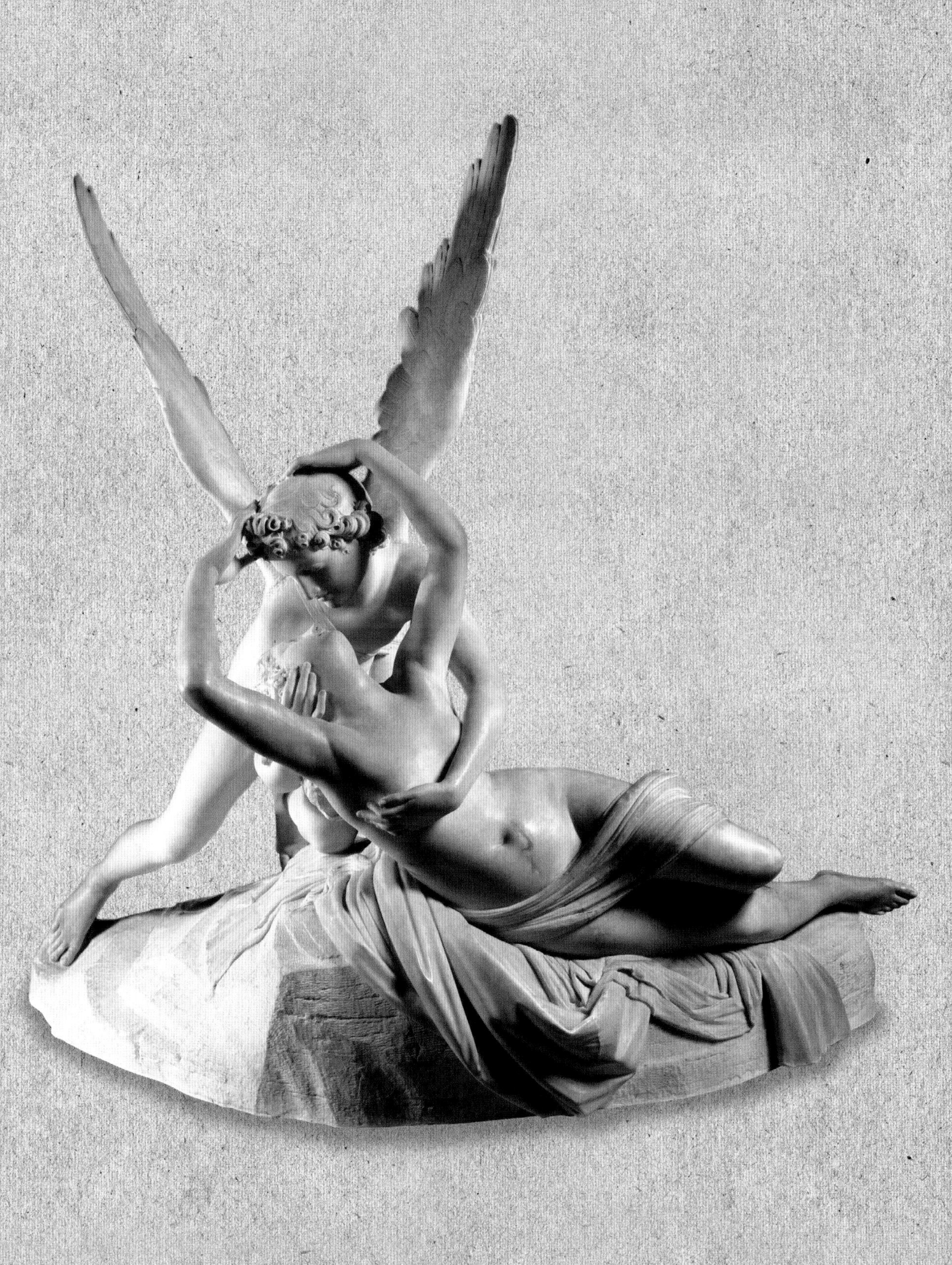

THE VALPINÇON BATHER

JEAN-AUGUSTE-DOMINIQUE INGRES
(1780–1867)

the 30-second artwork

The young Ingres painted this
sensual image of a female nude in 1808, while
studying at the French Academy in Rome.
Framed at the left by a curtain, a bather sits
cross-legged on the edge of a dishevelled bed
before a spouting font. Wearing nothing but a
red and white turban, her left arm only partially
clad in a bedsheet, she turns away from the
viewer. This pose allowed Ingres to emphasize
areas of her body which she herself cannot see
but which we, the viewer, can. Our voyeuristic
gaze, and our proximity to the bather, intensifies
the immediacy and the intimacy of the scene.
Ingres's decision to show the bather turbaned
and from behind transgressed the norms of
representing the female nude. As part of his
studentship in Rome, Ingres was required to
send the painting back to Paris to be judged by
a panel at the Académie de Beaux-Arts. Yet the
panel deemed the subject too close to a life
study. Devoid of historical references, they also
saw the painting as lacking in 'the beautiful
character of antiquity and with the grand and
noble style' that could be expected of an
Academy student. Such deviations from the
academic 'grand style' would rile the French art
establishment for the rest of Ingres's career.

*Ingres presents a highly
sensual image of a
female bather turned
from the viewer's gaze.*

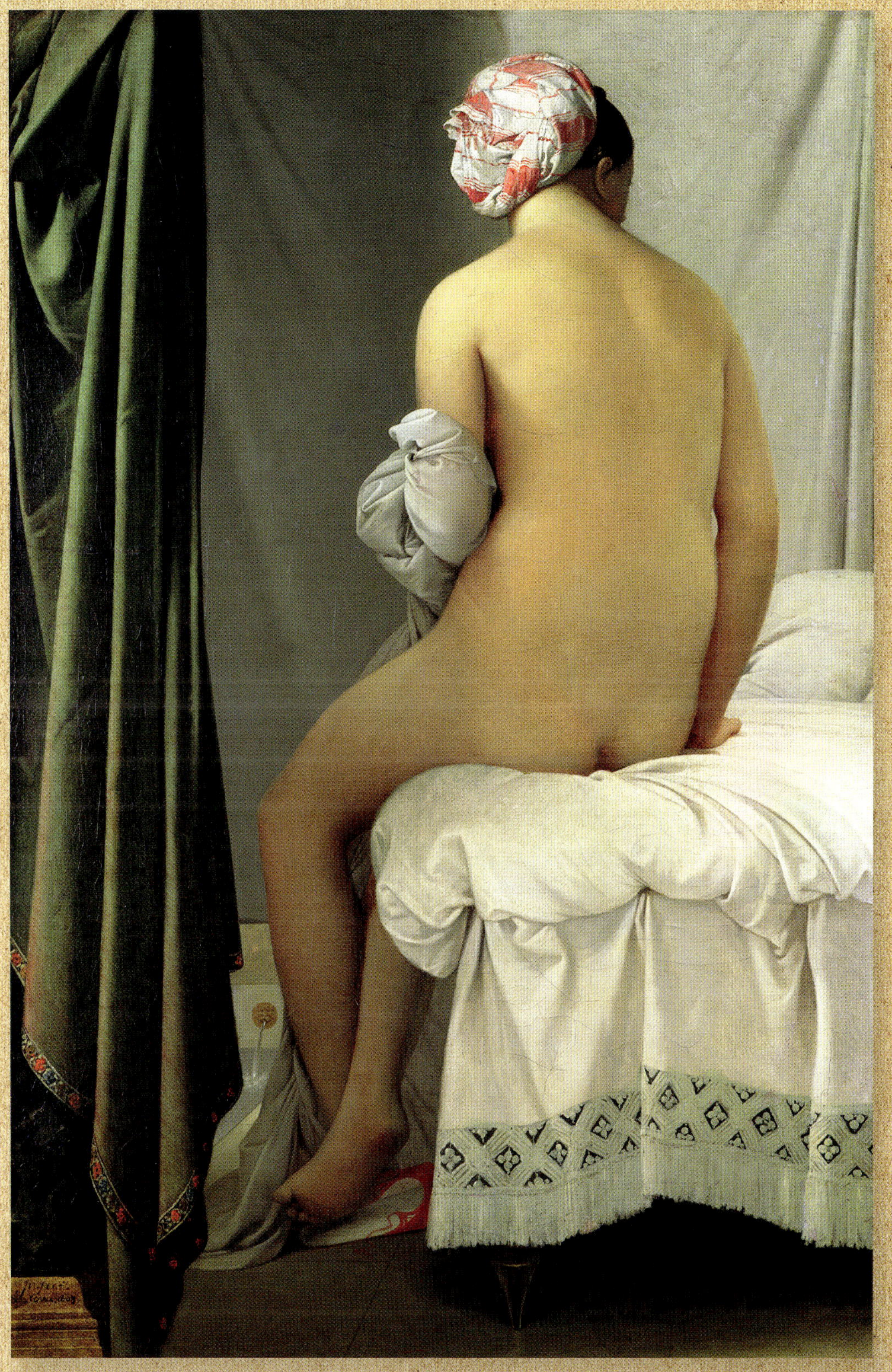

the 30-second artwork

Goya's harrowing masterpiece

commemorates an atrocity in Spanish history which took place on 3 May 1808: the execution of Madrilenian patriots by Napoleon Bonaparte's firing squad in retribution for their uprising against French occupation of Spain. This exceptionally large painting gives us the tense moment just before a group of patriots is shot by French soldiers on the Príncipe Pío, a hill just outside Madrid. The soldiers line up to the right, their faces turned from view, their bayoneted rifles ready to shoot. To the left, and flanked by men who cover their faces or cower in terror, one of the patriots holds up his arms in a moving plea for their lives. His bright white shirt and ochre trousers are illuminated by the slanted light of the soldiers' lamp, which simultaneously highlights the blood and bodies of his fallen comrades on the ground; here we are witnessing the second round of executions. Goya painted *The Third of May* six years after the uprising and the brutal occupation that followed. By that point, the French had been driven out and the Bourbon monarchy restored. However, the new king of Spain, Ferdinand VII, launched a tumultuous reign of terror. Goya's painting therefore points as much towards fresh atrocities as to those of the recent past.

3-SECOND SKETCH
With raw intensity, *The Third of May* commemorates the Spanish resistance to Napoleon's armies during the French occupation of 1808.

3-MINUTE STUDY
As a companion piece to *The Third of May*, Goya painted *The Second of May*, which portrays a violent scene in Madrid's city centre where Madrilenian patriots rose up against the Mamelukes, Turkish soldiers in Napoleon's French Army. Known as the *The Second of May 1808*, the picture shows the patriots on horseback in a moment of victory, a stark contrast to Goya's depiction of their appalling execution.

DETAILS OF THE WORK
Oil on canvas, 1814
268 x 347 cm (105½ x 136½ in)
Museo del Prado, Madrid

3-SECOND BIOGRAPHY
JOSEPH-NAPOLÉON BONAPARTE
1768–1844
The brother of Napoleon, installed as King of Spain, he was highly unpopular and smeared by opponents for alleged drunkenness, despite being teetotal

30-SECOND TEXT
Sarah Moulden

Goya documents the chilling execution of Spanish patriots by Napoleon's soldiers.

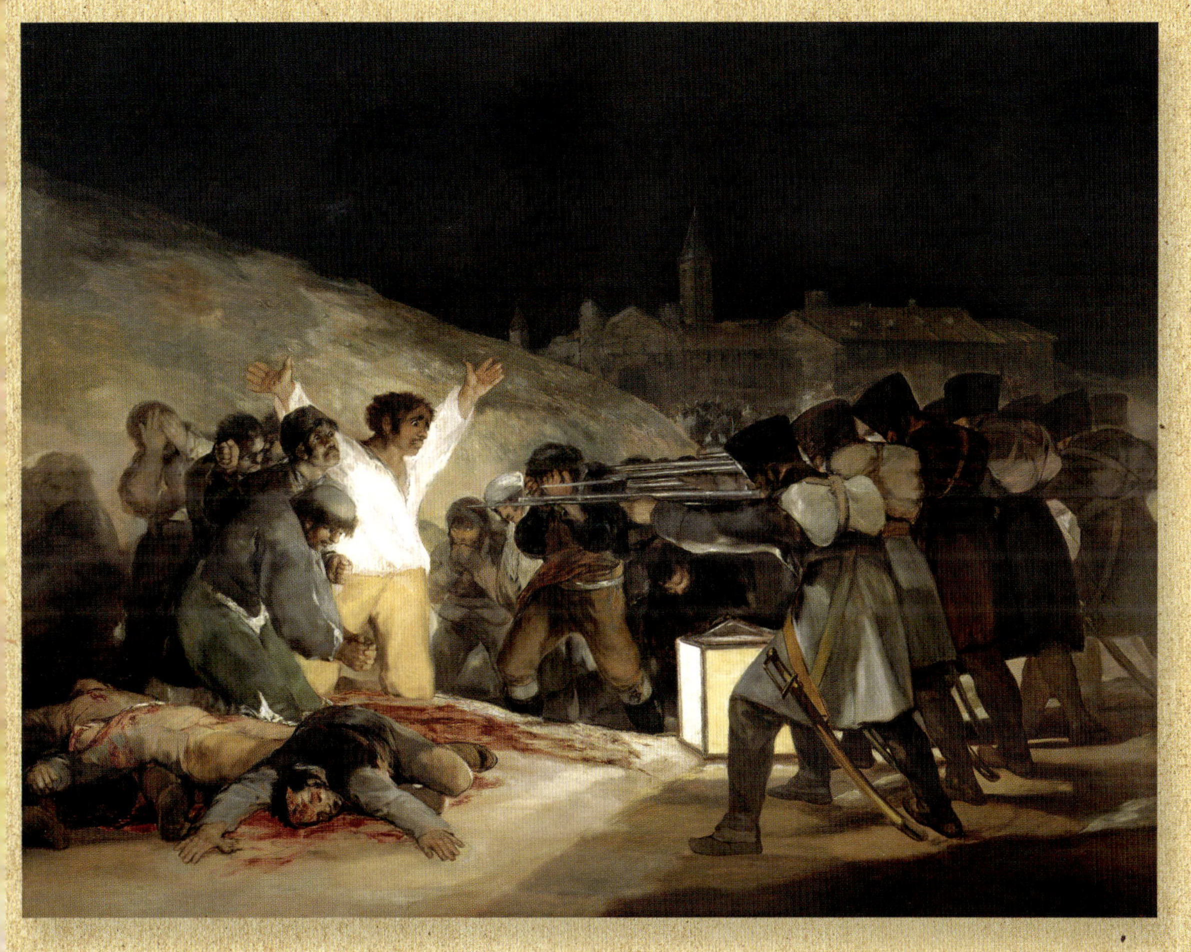

WANDERER ABOVE THE SEA OF FOG

CASPAR DAVID FRIEDRICH
(1774–1840)

the 30-second artwork

At the centre of Friedrich's painting, a solitary traveller stands on a rocky mountain summit surveying the awe-inspiring view before him. Facing out towards the horizon, this tall green-suited figure is silhouetted against the bright white of the fog-covered rocky precipices. All lines of sight converge at the traveller – the highest peak slopes down towards his head, the contours of the distant valley unite at his torso, and the rocks upon which he stands ascend towards his feet to raise him aloft – identifying this body as the key point of experience within the sublime landscape. With its emphasis on one man and his relationship with nature, *Wanderer above the Sea of Fog* firmly inhabits the Romantic imagination of the early nineteenth century, one that privileged the individual's subjective approach to beauty. Friedrich frequently employed the motif of a prominently-placed figure shown from behind, a device known as *Rückenfigur*, emphasizing the individual's private, incomplete view of the world. Indeed, with his front turned from view, the traveller's emotional response to the world he encounters on the mountain top is left unclear. Yet we can infer a sense of what he is feeling through his assured and upright stance, which indicates an invigorating personal experience.

From the top of a mountain, a solitary traveller communes with nature and with himself.

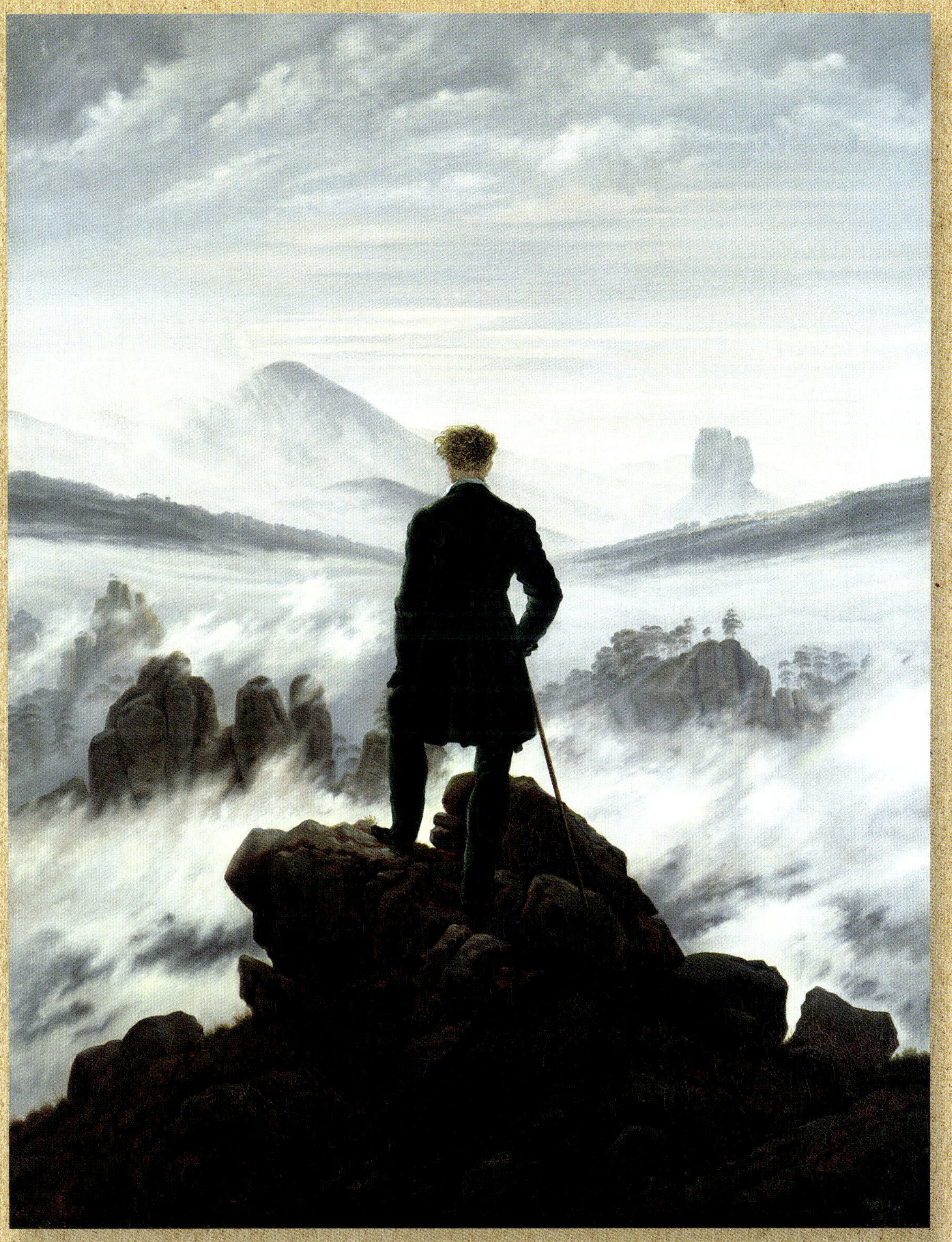

1768
The Royal Academy is founded by Royal Charter with the purpose of establishing 'a society for promoting the Arts of Design' in Britain

1769–90
The first president, Joshua Reynolds, delivers his fifteen *Discourses on Art* to the School's pupils, arguing that painters should not slavishly copy nature but attain an ideal form through study of the Old Masters, casts after the antique and the life study

1769
The first exhibition of contemporary art opens on Pall Mall, running from 25 April until 27 May

1771
The Academy moves to Old Somerset House, then a royal palace

1775
Architect Sir William Chambers wins the commission to design the new Somerset House

1780
The Academy occupies Chambers' new purpose-built apartments, complete with spaces for the School, its collection and library, and the Summer Exhibition

1837
The Academy moves to Trafalgar Square, sharing the premises with the newly established National Gallery

1860
The painter Laura Herford becomes the school's first woman student

1867
The Academy moves to Burlington House in Piccadilly, where it remains to this day

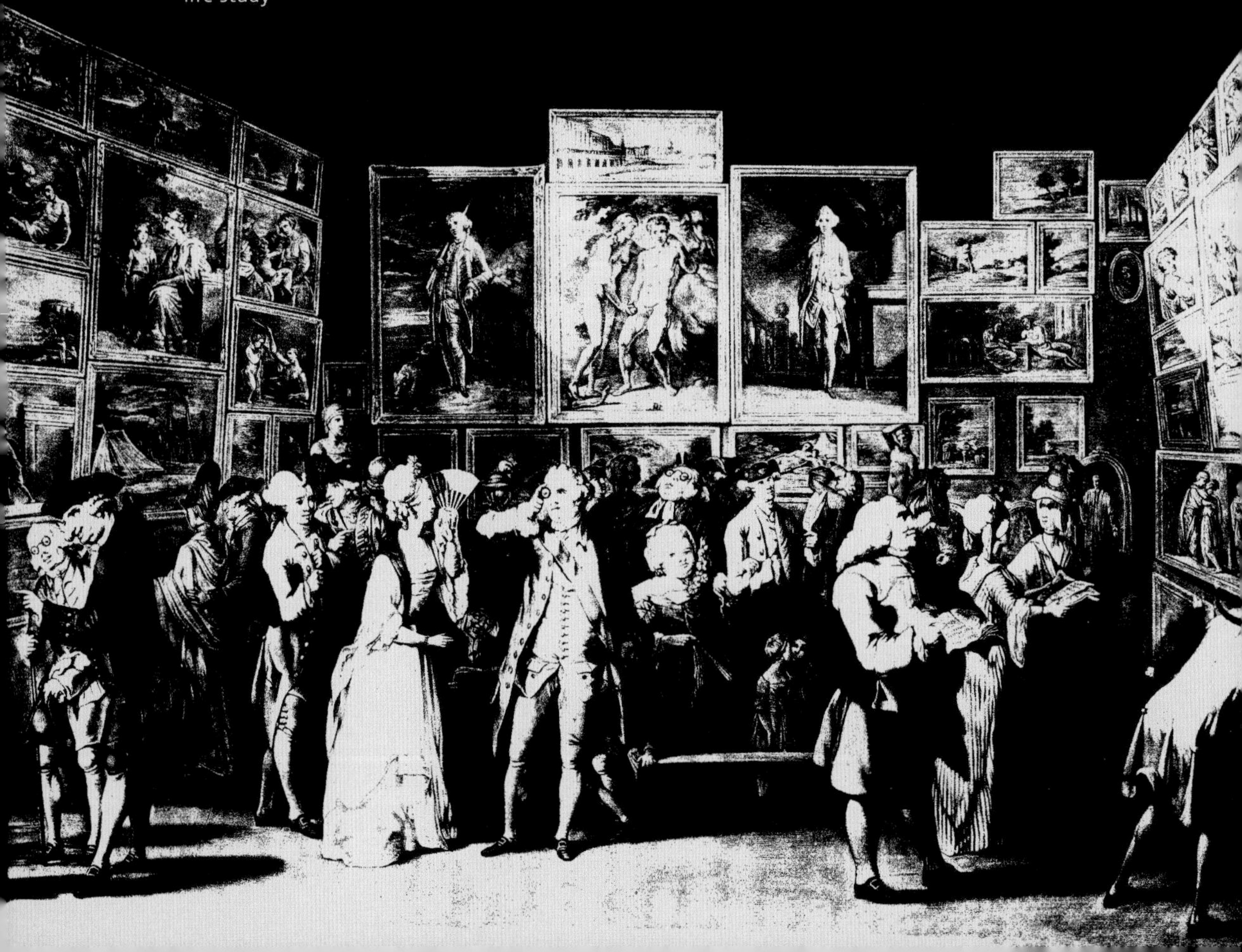

THE ROYAL ACADEMY OF ARTS, LONDON

Until the mid-eighteenth century, Britain had no official training school or exhibiting institution for its artists. All that changed, however, in 1768 with the founding of the Royal Academy in London. Designed to train artists and stage an annual exhibition of contemporary art, it transformed the conditions for artists and a growing public that loved art. 'The Exhibition', as it was known, soon became one of London's most fashionable events.

Initially based in rented rooms on Pall Mall, the Academy soon moved to sumptuous purpose-built apartments at Somerset House on the Strand, where it remained until moving down the road to Trafalgar Square in 1837. Somerset House accommodated the Academy's teaching spaces, a library and collection of sculptural casts, as well as a suite of exhibition rooms including a large top-floor gallery called the 'Great Room'. Each spring and early summer, works of art were hung in a dense floor-to-ceiling arrangement for marvelling crowds who paid a one-shilling entrance fee. Here artists' reputations were made and broken by vociferous critics whose reviews were readily consumed by a growing artistic readership.

The Academy rapidly defined itself as the home of artistic excellence in Britain. Its annual exhibitions provided an arena for ambitious assertions of artistic authority with exhibitors competing for both popular and critical acclaim. Distinctive compositions and eye-catching techniques from the likes of Joshua Reynolds, the Academy's first president, were designed to stand out from the patchwork of paintings on the walls, capturing the imagination of the audience below. Later, J. M. W. Turner's bold use of colour and bravura application of paint grabbed the attention of punters who by and large took the view that such qualities were employed mostly 'for the sake of singularity'.

The Royal Academy was instrumental in raising the social profile of artists in Britain. By exercising a virtual monopoly over artistic training and encouraging increasing numbers of young practitioners to try for entry year on year, it gave a great deal of currency to the artist's career. Today the Academy is still at the forefront of British artistic life, both as an important training centre for artists and as a major public gallery with a varied programme of exhibitions across the entire history of art.

Sarah Moulden

SALISBURY CATHEDRAL FROM THE BISHOP'S GROUND

JOHN CONSTABLE (1776–1837)

the 30-second artwork

This large painting of 1823, *Salisbury Cathedral from the Bishop's Ground,* shows the cathedral from the south-west, its famous spire – the tallest in England – piercing a bright blue, cloud-filled sky. In the foreground, bowed tree branches frame the scene and shelter the grazing cows beneath, while to the left a well-to-do couple – the bishop and his wife – stroll along a path, the bishop gesturing towards the magnificent cathedral over which he presides. With its expressive handling of paint and close observation of nature and medieval architecture, *Salisbury Cathedral* exhibits the full gamut of qualities that many contemporary art critics celebrated in British landscape painting. However, the work did not appeal to everyone, including the bishop himself who commissioned it. He disliked the dark raincloud encroaching onto the composition at the right and demanded a sunnier sky. Constable acquiesced and quickly produced two brighter versions – one the bishop presented to his daughter upon her marriage and another he would keep for himself. The original found a replacement buyer in the bishop's nephew, John Fisher, but insolvency forced Fisher to sell it back to Constable, leaving him stuck with the enormous canvas.

3-SECOND SKETCH

Salisbury Cathedral was the subject of a series of drawings and paintings that occupied John Constable for more than twenty years.

3-MINUTE STUDY

At a time when gothic buildings were entering public consciousness as never before, Constable's painting fed a contemporary desire for picturesque images of Britain's medieval past. Nonetheless, it was Salisbury's celebrated architectural detail that Constable claimed to have had greatest difficulty in depicting, even if he was ultimately happy with the result, declaring, 'My Cathedral looks very well. Indeed I got through that job uncommonly well considering how much I dreaded it.'

DETAILS OF THE WORK

Oil on canvas, 1823
87.6 x 111.8 cm (34½ x 44 in)
Victoria & Albert Museum, London

3-SECOND BIOGRAPHY

JOHN FISHER
1788–1832

Important influence in Constable's development of the large, attention-grabbing landscape paintings for which the artist is now best known

30-SECOND TEXT

Sarah Moulden

This is one of six finished paintings that Constable produced of Salisbury Cathedral.

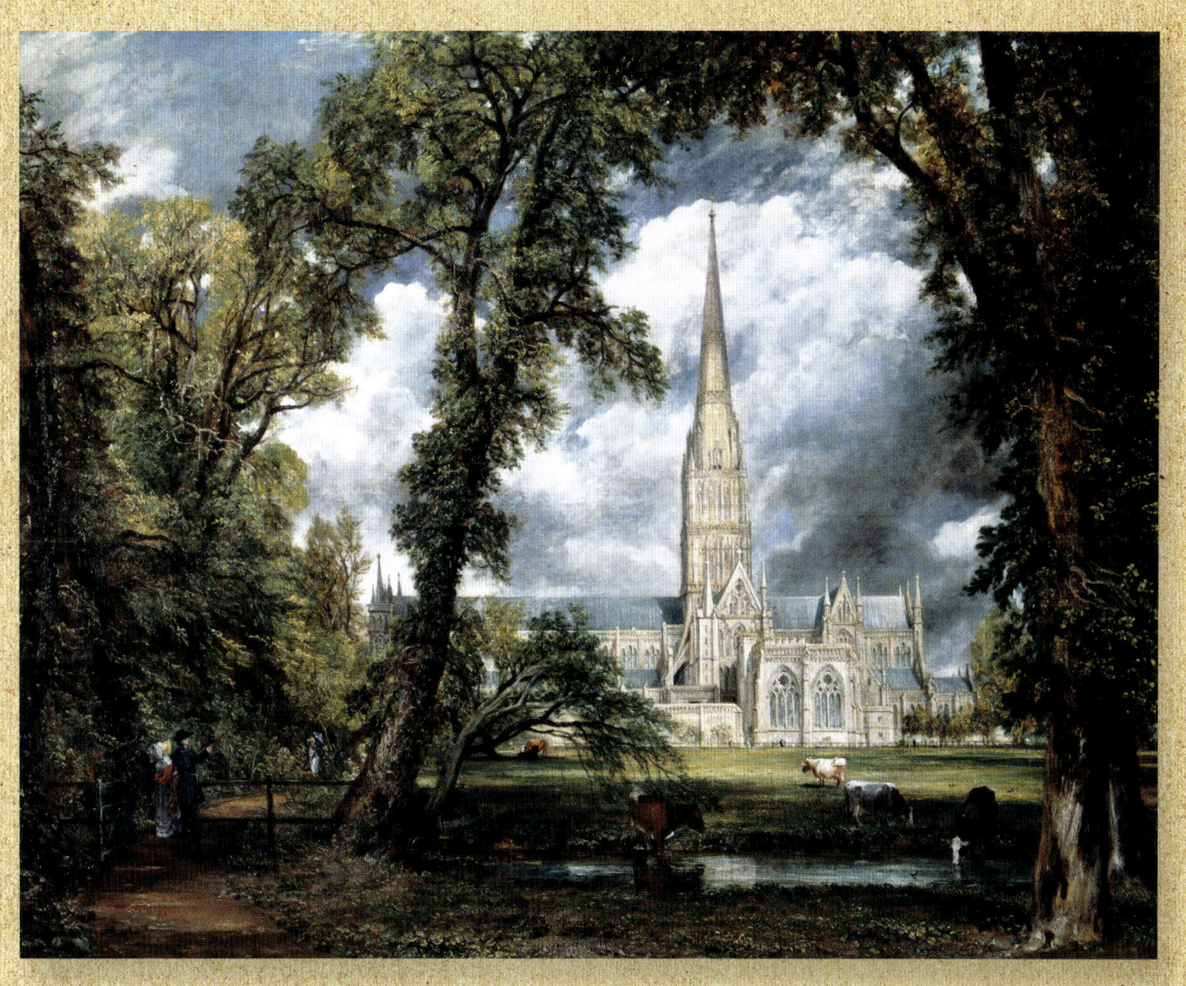

RAIN, STEAM AND SPEED – THE GREAT WESTERN RAILWAY

J. M. W. TURNER (1775–1851)

the 30-second artwork

A steam train hurtles along a dramatically foreshortened diagonal of rail track towards the edge of the picture plane. The blurriness of the emerging carriages indicates it does so at extreme pace. As the title of Turner's painting denotes, this work is about the speed of rail travel, whatever the weather, a theme reinforced in formal terms by its bold execution. Swirls and smudges of paint envelop the train, its bright white headlight blazing through a vortex of rain that blends into a misty haze of steam. Barely detectable at the bottom right of the picture, a hare (a symbol of speed) darts across the track. Here modernity meets tradition as the train forcefully displaces nature. Despite the work's painterly obscurity, the train's location can be precisely identified as the Maidenhead Viaduct, a recently constructed bridge across the River Thames between Taplow and Maidenhead. This formed part of the route of the Great Western Railway, the most ambitious railway project of the day. *Rain, Steam and Speed* was itself regarded as highly ambitious by the critics who saw it at the Royal Academy in 1844. The *Morning Chronicle* was simultaneously baffled and delighted by Turner's technique, describing the work as both 'the most insane and the most magnificent' of the artist's submissions to the show that year.

DETAILS OF THE WORK
Oil on canvas, 1844
91 x 121.8 cm (35¾ x 48 in)
National Gallery, London

3-SECOND BIOGRAPHY
ISAMBARD KINGDOM BRUNEL
1806–59
Pioneering chief engineer of the Great Western Railway, designer of numerous bridges, tunnels, dockyards, railway stations and ships

30-SECOND TEXT
Sarah Moulden

In Turner's dramatic painting, an onrushing steam train cuts across the pastoral world.

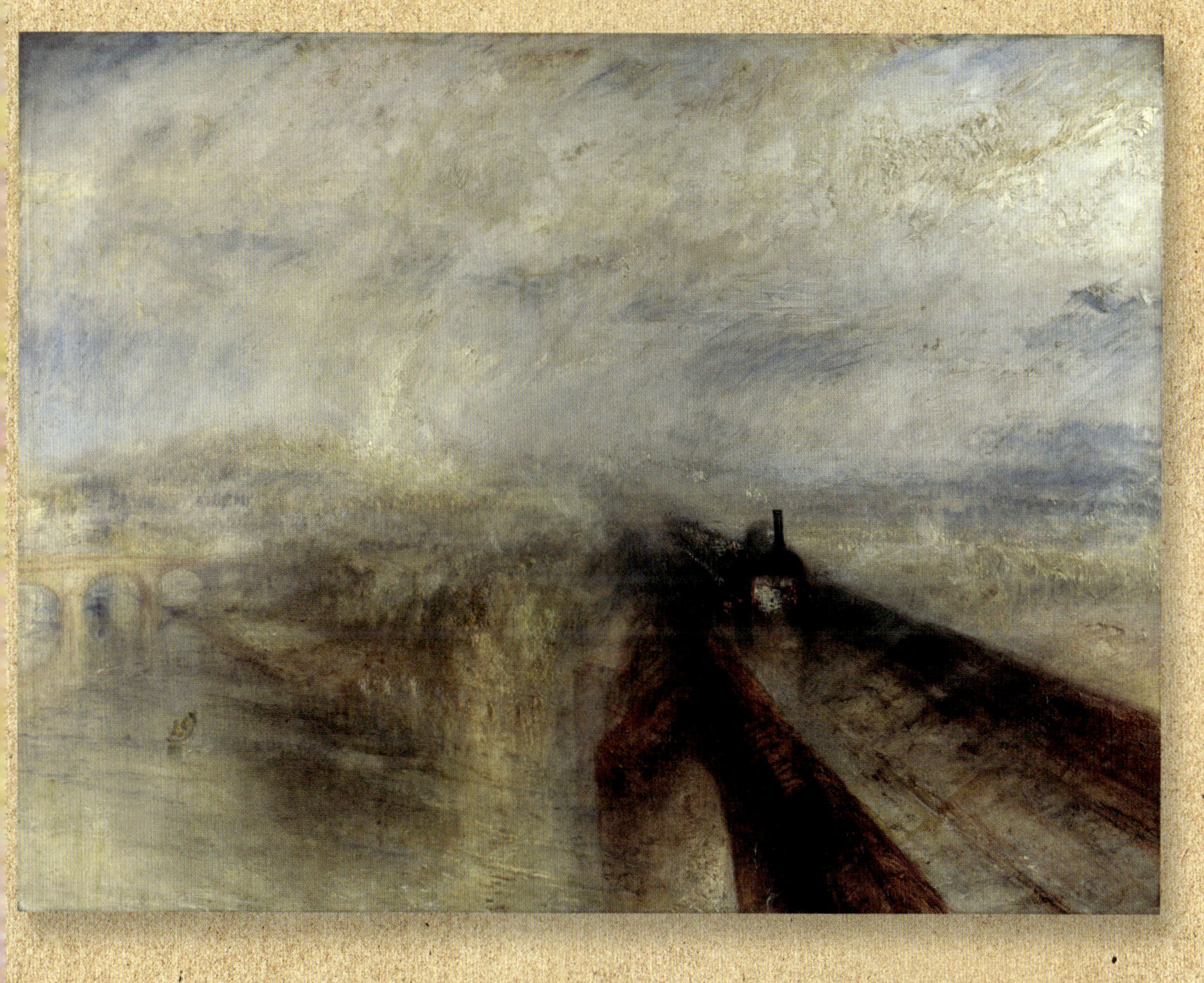

REALISM, IMPRESSIONISM
& POST-IMPRESSIONISM

Academic art Type of painting that follows the conventions and principles of the official Academies of painting and sculpture established across Europe from the seventeenth to the nineteenth century, for example, The Royal Academy in London, or the Académie des Beaux-Arts, Paris.

avant-garde Challenging orthodoxies and traditions in art, culture and wider society, and attempting to disrupt the status quo. In relation to art, this can be manifest through radical statements or actions, or innovative use of materials and techniques.

casting The process of making a sculpture, or other three-dimensional object, by pouring liquid metal, often bronze, into a mould. On cooling, the metal solidifies, and the cast (sculpture) can be removed from the mould.

en plein air The practice of painting out of doors, most often associated with landscape painting. This was a form of working that became popular in the nineteenth century, and was particularly espoused by the Impressionists.

facture The characteristic manner in which an individual artist handles the medium in which they work.

Impressionism Influential art movement originating in France in the 1870s. Artists associated with the group, which included Monet, Renoir and Manet, aimed to capture in paint the transient quality of light and its effects on the changing appearance of colour and form in nature.

Modernism Overarching term applied to artists and movements from the mid nineteenth century to the late 1960s who set out to reinvigorate art through the introduction of new subjects, forms and techniques. Although not mutually exclusive, while some artists produced works that engaged with contemporary life – often viewing art as a vehicle for social change – others were more concerned with the material and formal qualities of their medium, which would lead to the predominance of abstraction.

motif The subject of a painting, or a distinct element within its composition or design.

narrative A story conveyed by an artwork.

nocturne A musical term meaning 'night piece', which can be applied to a painting of a night scene.

palette The tray on which colours are set out and mixed by an artist. The term, by association, is also applied to the range of colours used by an artist in a painting.

Paris Salon The official annual exhibition of the Académie des Beaux-Arts in Paris, and the principal public display of fine art in France during the late eighteenth and nineteenth centuries. More progressive artists often viewed it as too conservative, and alternative Salons were established from the 1860s onwards, including those organized by the Impressionists.

Post-Impressionist A general term applied to progressive artists of the late nineteenth and early twentieth century that did not adhere to the principles of Impressionism, including Cezanne, van Gogh and Gauguin. The term was coined by the British art critic Roger Fry in the title of an exhibition including these artists in 1910.

still life A genre of painting that depicts an arrangement of inanimate natural or manufactured objects. Throughout the history of art items have been painted for their symbolic meaning, although modern artists have tended to use them as neutral subjects in order to forefront the formal qualities of their work.

tympanum The area above a lintel formed by an enclosing arch or frame.

woodblock print A type of print made by cutting a design in relief into a block of wood. The inked block is pressed onto the paper or cloth producing a mirror image of the design.

the 30-second artwork

This vividly coloured painting

depicts an impoverished blind girl and her sister resting after a storm; it comments directly on Victorian attitudes towards disability and vagrancy. A child prodigy, Millais enrolled at the Royal Academy Schools aged 11, their youngest ever student. In 1848, with fellow pupils William Holman Hunt (1827–1910) and Dante Gabriel Rossetti (1828–1882), he formed the Pre-Raphaelite Brotherhood, directly challenging the Academy's teachings and influence on mid-nineteenth century art. The 'Pity the Blind' tag around the girl's neck and the accordion in her lap remind the viewer of the girl's destitution and her reliance on charity. The double rainbow in the background heightens the pathos of the scene: while her sister turns to look, the blind girl cannot appreciate its beauty. Yet the painting is filled with a myriad of symbol and suggestion conveying her other, heightened senses. Sitting quietly immersed, the girl's rich sensory experience is conveyed through the suggestion of sound from the crows and cows in the field behind; the warmth of the sun to which she lifts her face; the smell of rain and grass after the storm as indicated in the purple-blue sky; and the feeling of touch through the blind girl's hands, one caressing a blade of grass, the other clasped tightly in her sister's hand.

3-SECOND SKETCH
Poignantly contrasting the viewer's appreciation of a brilliant rural scene with the blind girl's own experience, Millais provokes contemplation of the act of seeing itself.

3-MINUTE STUDY
The Pre-Raphaelite Brotherhood formed in September 1848 at Millais' home on Gower Street in London. Rejecting the teachings of the Royal Academy, which idealized Raphael as the greatest example its students could emulate, they looked to earlier artists such as Giotto, Jan van Eyck and Fra Angelico for a spiritually attuned art with emphasis on purity of line and clarity of colour. They are widely considered the first British avant-garde art group.

DETAILS OF THE WORK
Oil on canvas, 1856
82.6 x 62.2 cm (32½ x 24½ in)
Birmingham Museum and Art Gallery

3-SECOND BIOGRAPHY
JOHN RUSKIN
1819–1900
Among the most influential of Victorian art critics, a fervent early supporter of the Pre-Raphaelites and champion of what he called their 'truth to nature'

30-SECOND TEXT
Maria Alambritis

The resting butterfly on the blind girl's cape conveys her stillness, absorbed in sensation.

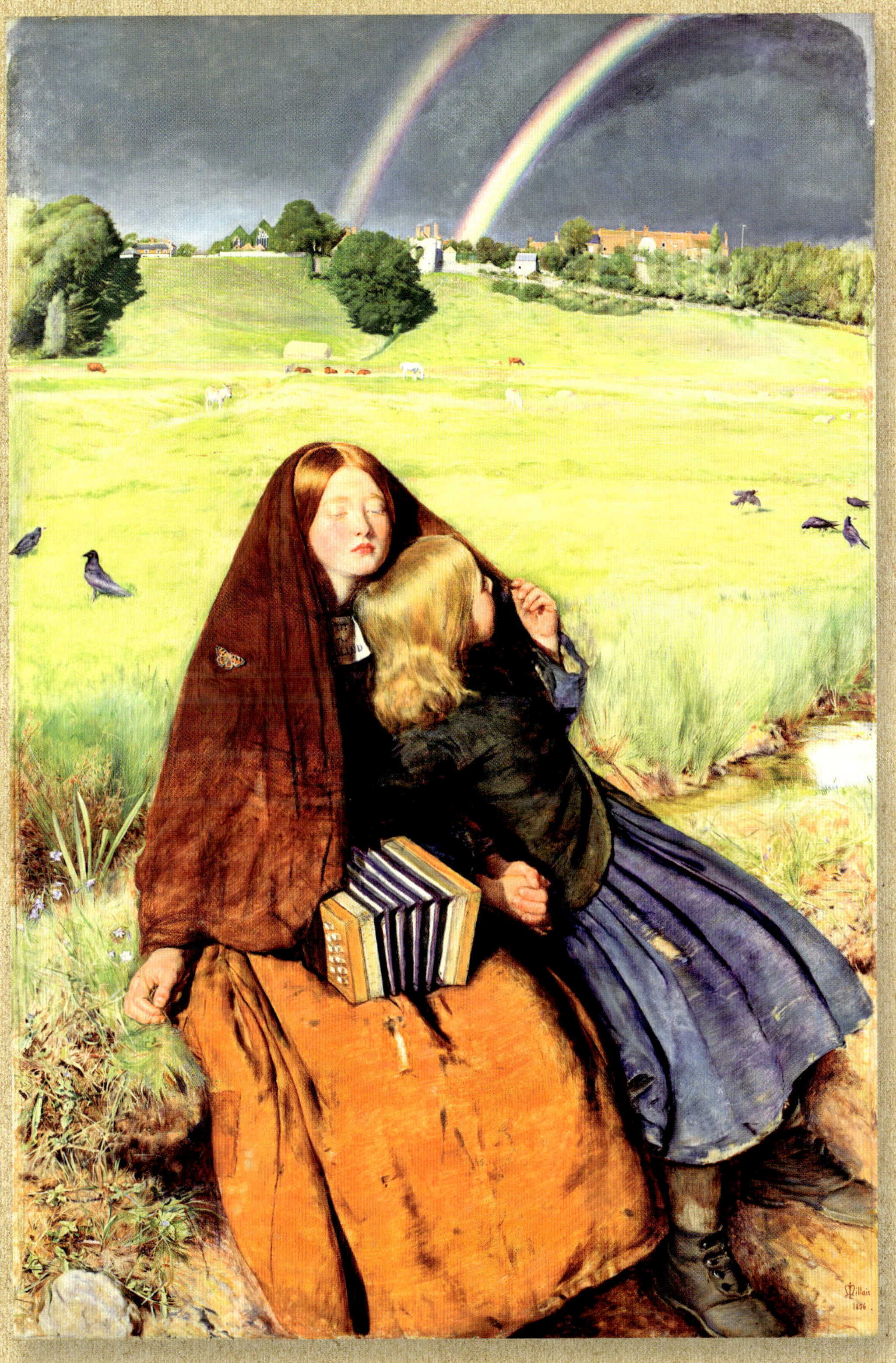

the 30-second artwork

This figure was originally called *The Poet* and intended to crown the tympanum of Rodin's *Gates of Hell*, a commission for a set of bronze doors for the museum of decorative arts in Paris. Though the doors were never cast in Rodin's lifetime, he reworked and exhibited individual figures from the *Gates* separately over the course of his career. First exhibited as *The Thinker* in 1888, it was after being enlarged in around 1903 that this figure came to be one of Rodin's most famous works and one of the most celebrated sculptures in Western art, reproduced in numerous casts and versions worldwide. Though inspired by the sculpture of classical Greece and the Italian Renaissance, Rodin rejected the idealized mythogical figures favoured by the art establishment of his day. Instead, he introduced a naturalistic treatment of the human form, in which the potential of the body to express the inner life of the subject was of paramount importance. The *Gates of Hell* was inspired by the poet Dante Alighieri's *Divine Comedy*, with this figure representing the poet himself, musing over his creation as the damned circled their way through hell. Hunched in intense contemplation, the furrowed brow and powerful body offer a timeless embodiment of the human struggle with the deepest questions of existence.

3-SECOND SKETCH
With its lack of narrative context, Rodin's *Thinker* resists characterization. Instead we are drawn to the intense but unseen drama of his mind.

3-MINUTE STUDY
The Thinker was originally a small figure about 70 cm (27½ in) high. Continually recasting his works in different poses, sizes and media, Rodin pioneered a new way of sculpting in which the work was not static but open to numerous interpretations. The nudity and monumental size of *The Thinker* convey a universal, timeless quality. Rodin said of this work, 'My idea was to represent the man as a symbol of humanity, a robust, workman-like figure'.

DETAILS OF THE WORK
Bronze, 1880 & later
Various

3-SECOND BIOGRAPHY
DANTE ALIGHIERI
1265–1321
Italian poet whose best-known work, *La divina commedia* (*The Divine Comedy*), takes the protagonist on a journey through hell, purgatory and finally paradise

30-SECOND TEXT
Maria Alambritis

The powerful modelling of the muscles shows the influence of Michelangelo, whom Rodin greatly admired.

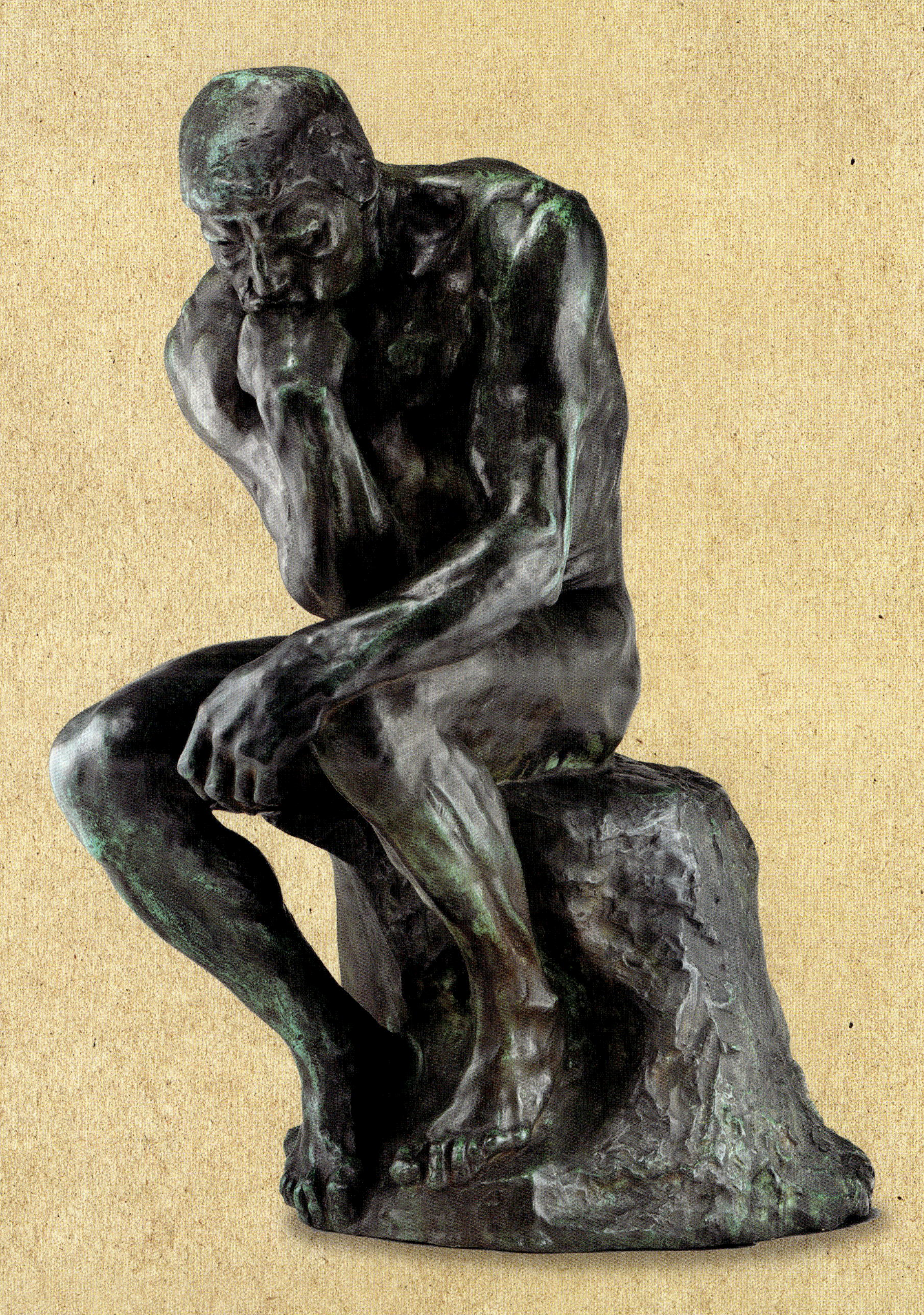

A BAR AT THE FOLIES-BERGÈRE

ÉDOUARD MANET (1832–83)

the 30-second artwork

Painted just before he died, this is one of Manet's masterpieces from a series depicting the lively interiors of late nineteenth-century Paris cafes, concert halls and bars. Manet broke with the conventions of Academic painting and caused scandal among the art establishment of his day, who saw his frank, boldly executed depictions of contemporary Parisian life as vulgar and distasteful. The Folies Bergère was one of the most popular cabaret music halls in Paris, infamous for the *demi-mondes*, or prostitutes, who frequented it. Providing the perfect setting for witnessing the 'spectacle' of modern life, it attracted people from across the social spectrum, including avant-garde painters and writers such as Manet, Émile Zola and Stéphane Mallarmé, whose experience of such places inspired their work. In this painting, the inscrutable gaze of the barmaid directly confronts us as she stands behind a marble-topped bar, its bottles, vases and fruit painted as carefully as in a still life. The mirror behind her reflects the crowded room, full of fashionably dressed clientele beneath the bright lights. Yet her reflection is shown too far to the right. This deliberate distortion of the conventions of composition and space was characteristic of Manet and is here presented in one of its most perplexing examples.

DETAILS OF THE WORK
Oil on canvas, 1881–82
96 x 130 cm (37¾ x 51¼ in)
Courtauld Gallery, London

3-SECOND BIOGRAPHY
ÉMILE ZOLA
1840–1902
French novelist and art critic, and the most influential exponent of literary naturalism, employing meticulous observations of the often sordid realities of everyday Parisian life

30-SECOND TEXT
Maria Alambritis

Manet's focus is on the barmaid, so the acrobat's feet dangling in the top left-hand corner are an incidental detail.

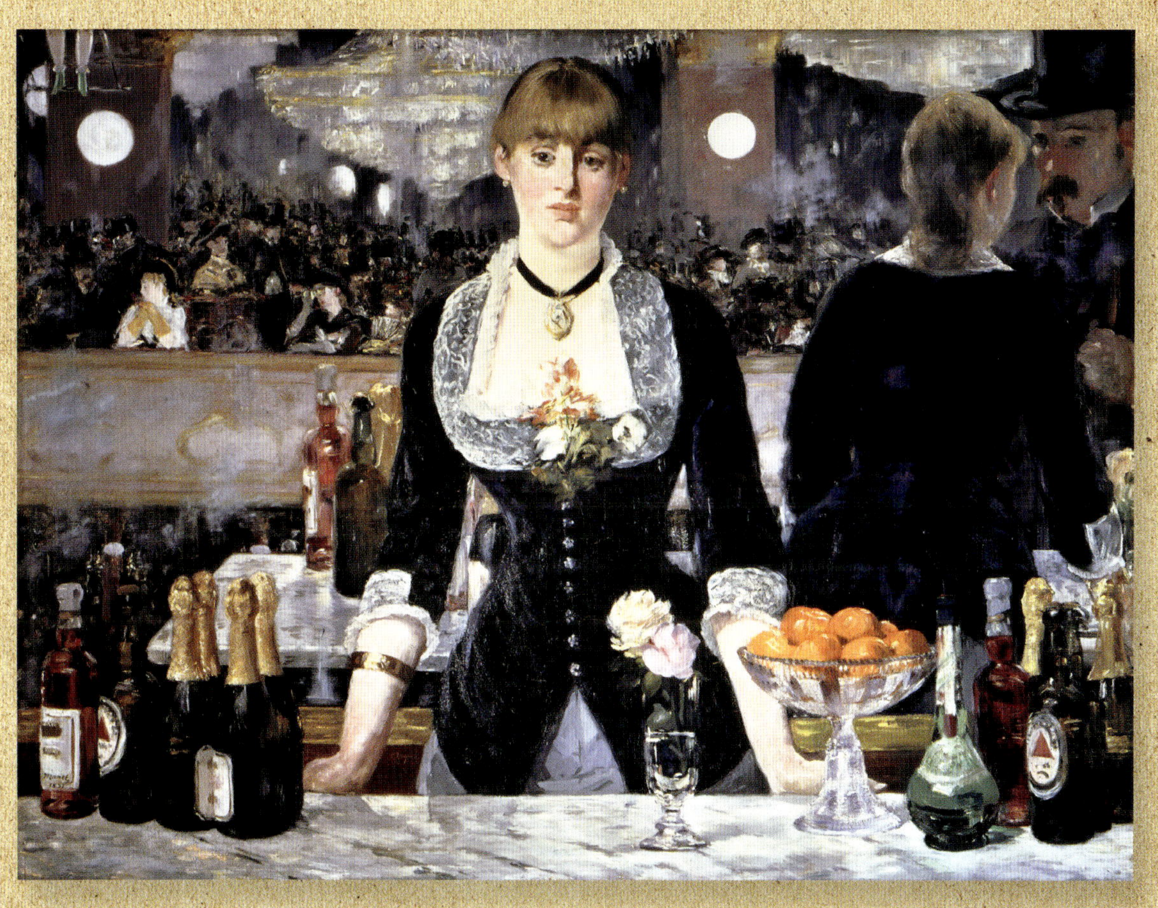

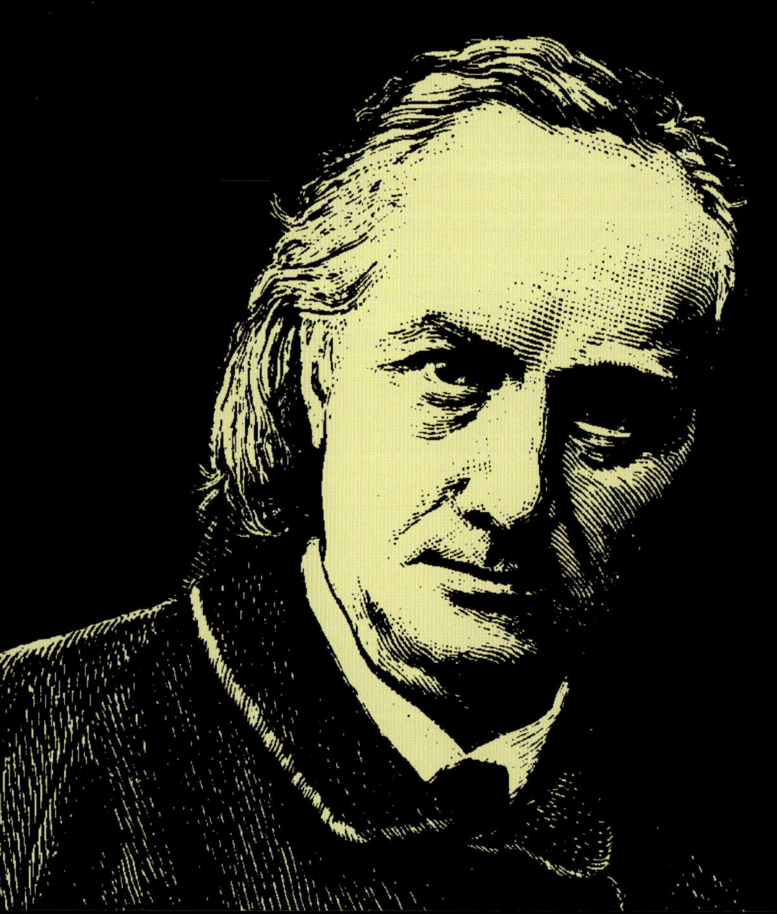

CHARLES BAUDELAIRE

'The painter, the true painter, will be he who can wring from contemporary life its epic aspect and make us see and understand, with colour or in drawing, how great and poetic we are in our cravats and our polished boots?' (*Salon de 1845*)

Charles Baudelaire lived in France at a time of tumultuous political, cultural and social change, witnessing both the 1848 Revolution and the 1851 coup. In his poetry and art criticism he sought to convey the experience of modern life through the image of the city of Paris itself.

Born in Paris in 1821, Baudelaire cultivated a love of painting from a young age and was fascinated with the connection between language and the visual arts. He believed the fleeting, ephemeral events of modern urban life were a worthy subject for art and that the role of the painter was to capture these moments and express their heroic and poetic nature.

Baudelaire felt true beauty existed among the crowds and boulevards, bars, cafes and theatres of Paris. In his seminal essay '*Le Peintre de la vie moderne*' (The Painter of Modern Life, 1863), Baudelaire set out his vision of the archetypal figure of the modern artist as *flâneur*, the well-dressed, voyeuristic dandy who roams the streets of Paris taking in the sights and scenes, remaining always aloof. This essay is often aligned with the artworks of the Impressionists that emerged over the following few decades.

His most important collection of poetry, *Les Fleurs du Mal* (The Flowers of Evil, 1857) expressed his view that beauty was not found in an ideal type or bound by moral concerns, but instead contingent on the historical moment and impressions made on the spectator. The poems also express Baudelaire's fascination with synaesthesia, the mingling of the senses. In its evocation of the pleasures of lust, alcohol, narcotic substances and the underbelly of Parisian life, the publication of these poems brought against Baudelaire charges of indecency and public offence leading to his notorious reputation as a depraved and decadent poet.

Elevating the themes of daily contemporary life to the status of the ideal subject matter for painting and poetry, his writings are now acknowledged as seminal to the development of Modernist thought.

THE STARRY NIGHT
VINCENT VAN GOGH (1853–90)

the 30-second artwork

Nature was an important source of inspiration for Van Gogh throughout his life, culminating in a series of landscapes he painted in 1889 while a resident at the Saint-Rémy asylum near Arles in the South of France. Seeking to capture the essence of his Provençal surroundings in the pre-dawn hours, in *Starry Night* he depicts a quiet village edged by towering cypress trees and sloping mountains, themselves dwarfed by a roiling sky of stars and clouds. Van Gogh's early paintings feature scenes of rural Dutch life in earthy browns and sombre blacks, but his move to Paris in 1886 brought a profound change to his work. Influenced by avant-garde artists such as Paul Gauguin, with whom he became friends, the Dutchman brightened his colour palette and began experimenting with texture and form. But when the frenetic pace of Parisian life took its toll on his physical and mental health, he moved south seeking respite. During his stay at Saint-Rémy he became fascinated with capturing nocturnal effects in paint. The view from his bedroom window offered an uninterrupted vista of the night sky. *Starry Night* uses some of Van Gogh's favourite motifs, such as stars and twilight, achieving an emotional intensity that even he seldom matched.

The church spire in the centre of the painting is more Dutch than Provençal in style.

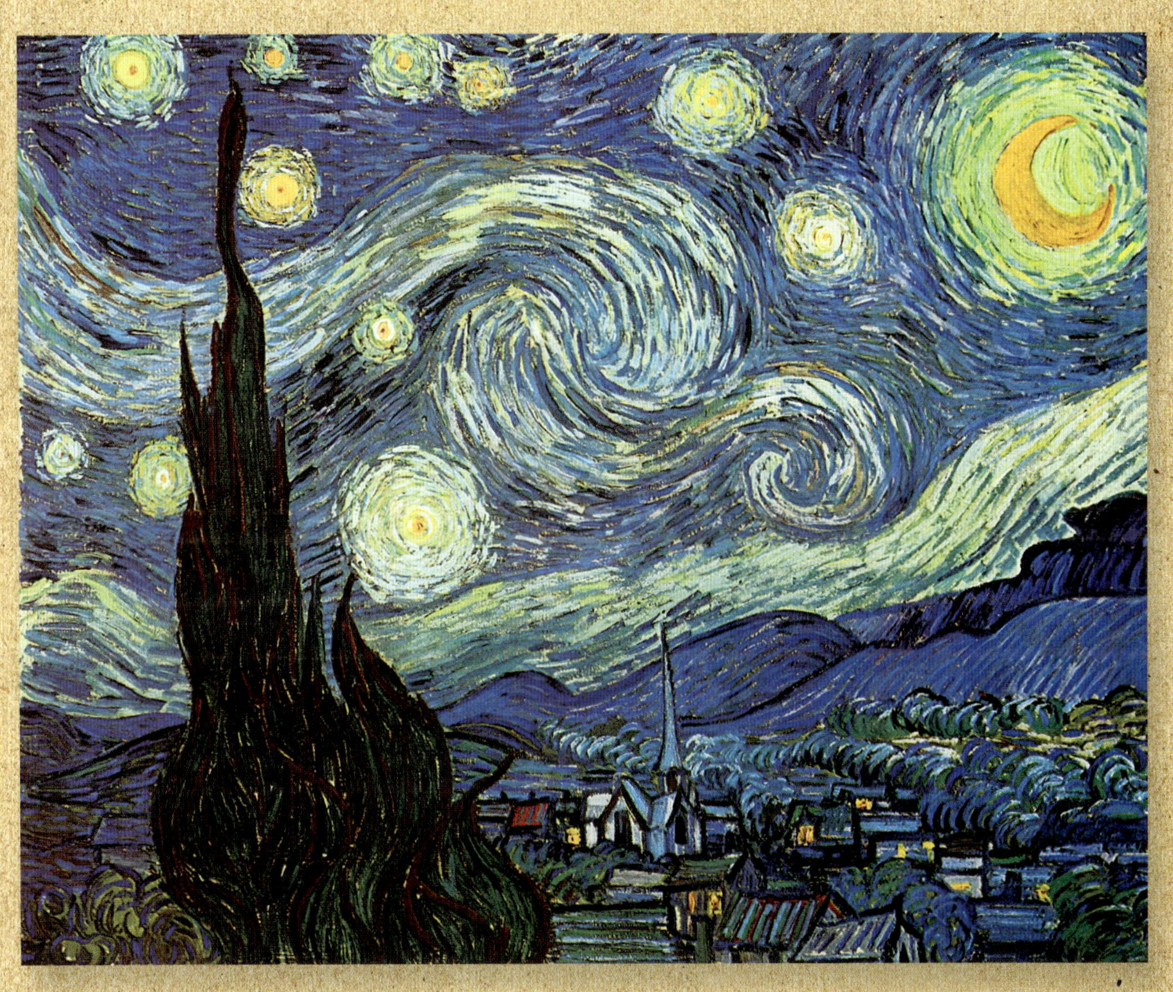

THE CHILD'S BATH
MARY CASSATT (1844–1926)

the 30-second artwork

While there were many women artists working in the latter part of the nineteenth century, historically their lives and careers have been overlooked. In 1877, Cassatt was invited by Edgar Degas to exhibit with the Impressionists instead of the annual Paris Salon. She gladly accepted, becoming the only American artist to show with the group, saying, 'at last I could work with complete independence without concerning myself with the eventual judgement of a jury … I hated conventional art. I began to live.' Working with the Impressionists allowed Cassatt to explore her favoured theme of the modern woman in various environments – at home, in the garden, at the theatre. From 1888 to 1914 her work focused predominantly on the subject of mother and child. Eschewing idealized depictions of motherhood, she instead portrayed mothers as capable and independent women. In this scene, Cassatt presents an intimate moment between mother and child. As the mother clasps the child around the waist, and presses her foot gently into the water, the child steadies herself on the mother's leg. The high viewpoint of this work enhances the feeling of a private moment. The viewer's attention is concentrated on the two figures, while they gaze downwards, emphasizing the interiority of the scene.

Pressing her thumb into her thigh, the child mimics the mother's gesture on her foot.

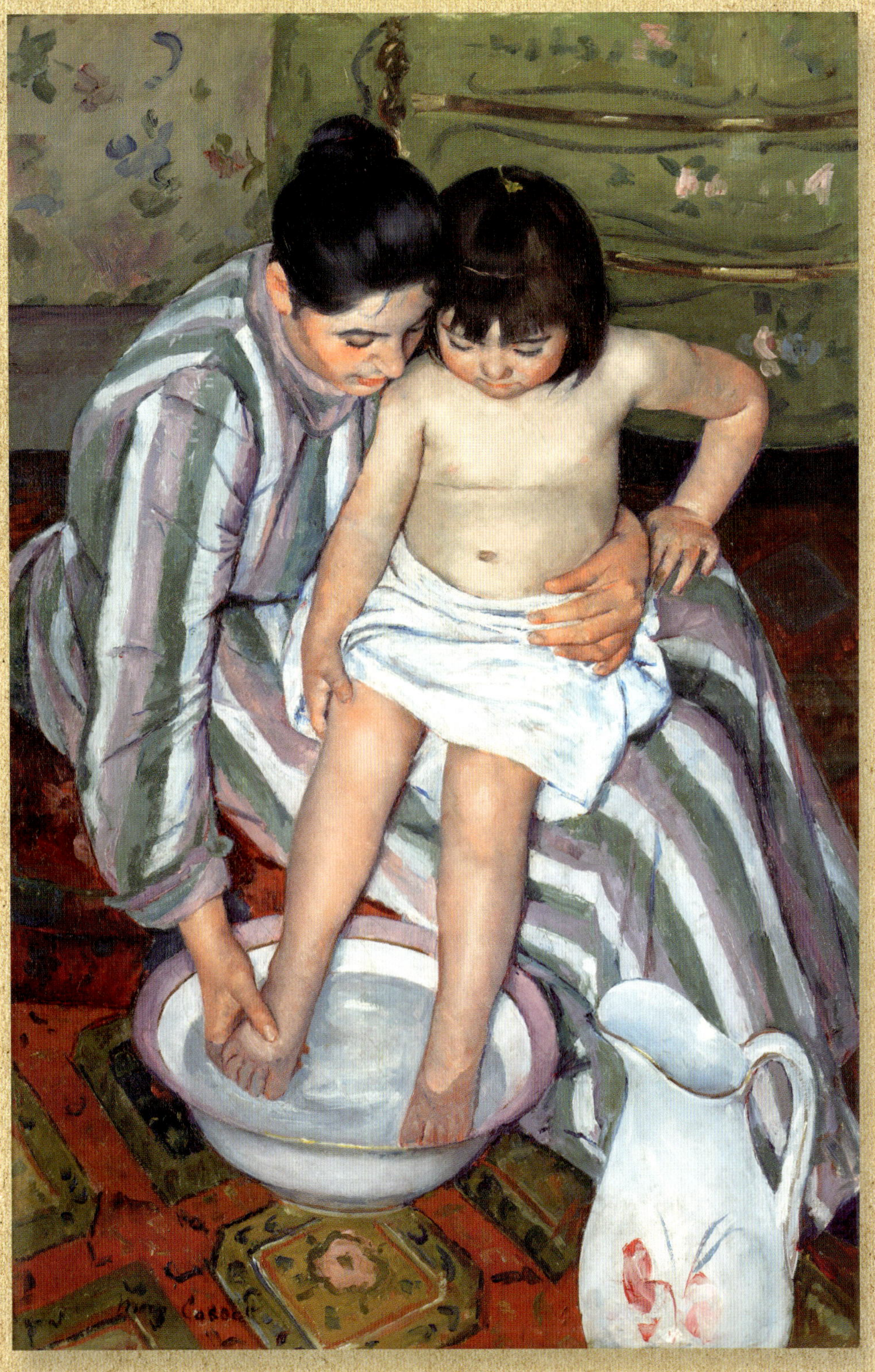

the 30-second artwork

Monet is acknowledged as the definitive painter of the group of artists known as the Impressionists. Often choosing to paint *en plein air*, the Impressionists aimed to capture the transient qualities of light and its varying effects on perceptions of colour and form. Throughout his career, Monet was preoccupied with how the appearance of a particular subject would change at different times of the day. This painting of the Gothic cathedral of Notre-Dame in Rouen is one of a series he created depicting the evanescent effects caused by the play of light and different atmospheric conditions on the cathedral façade. In a letter written from Rouen to his wife Alice, Monet observed, 'Everything changes, even if stone'. Monet visited Rouen twice, in 1892 and 1893, working from a milliner's shop overlooking the cathedral, usually on multiple canvases at the same time, each one depicting a different time of day. Eventually amassing more than thirty such views, he later reworked these paintings at his studio in Giverny, forming them into a unified set. In this version, the cathedral is shown in early morning; the glow of the new day is seen gathering in the sky above, illuminating the cathedral's topmost points, cascading down its west façade and chasing away the red-violet and dusky blue shadows loitering at the cathedral door.

3-SECOND SKETCH
The focus here is not Rouen cathedral itself, but how light, air, humidity and time of day transform the appearance of the subject.

3-MINUTE STUDY
Monet painted several subjects in series from the 1890s onwards, including grain stacks, poplars and London's Charing Cross Bridge. The Rouen cathedral series was among his most renowned, unique for its singular focus on a dramatic architectural form. Monet selected twenty canvases from the series, including this one, to be exhibited in May 1895 at the gallery of art dealer Paul Durand-Ruel. They caused a sensation and were seen as the essence of modernity.

DETAILS OF THE WORK
Oil on canvas, 1894
100.3 x 65 cm (30½ x 25⅝ in)
J. Paul Getty Museum,
Los Angeles

3-SECOND BIOGRAPHY
PAUL DURAND-RUEL
1831–1922
One of the most important art dealers of the late nineteenth century, who recognized the potential of the Impressionists and promoted their work

30-SECOND TEXT
Maria Alambritis

The highly textured paint surface embodies the cathedral's stone façade emerging in early morning light.

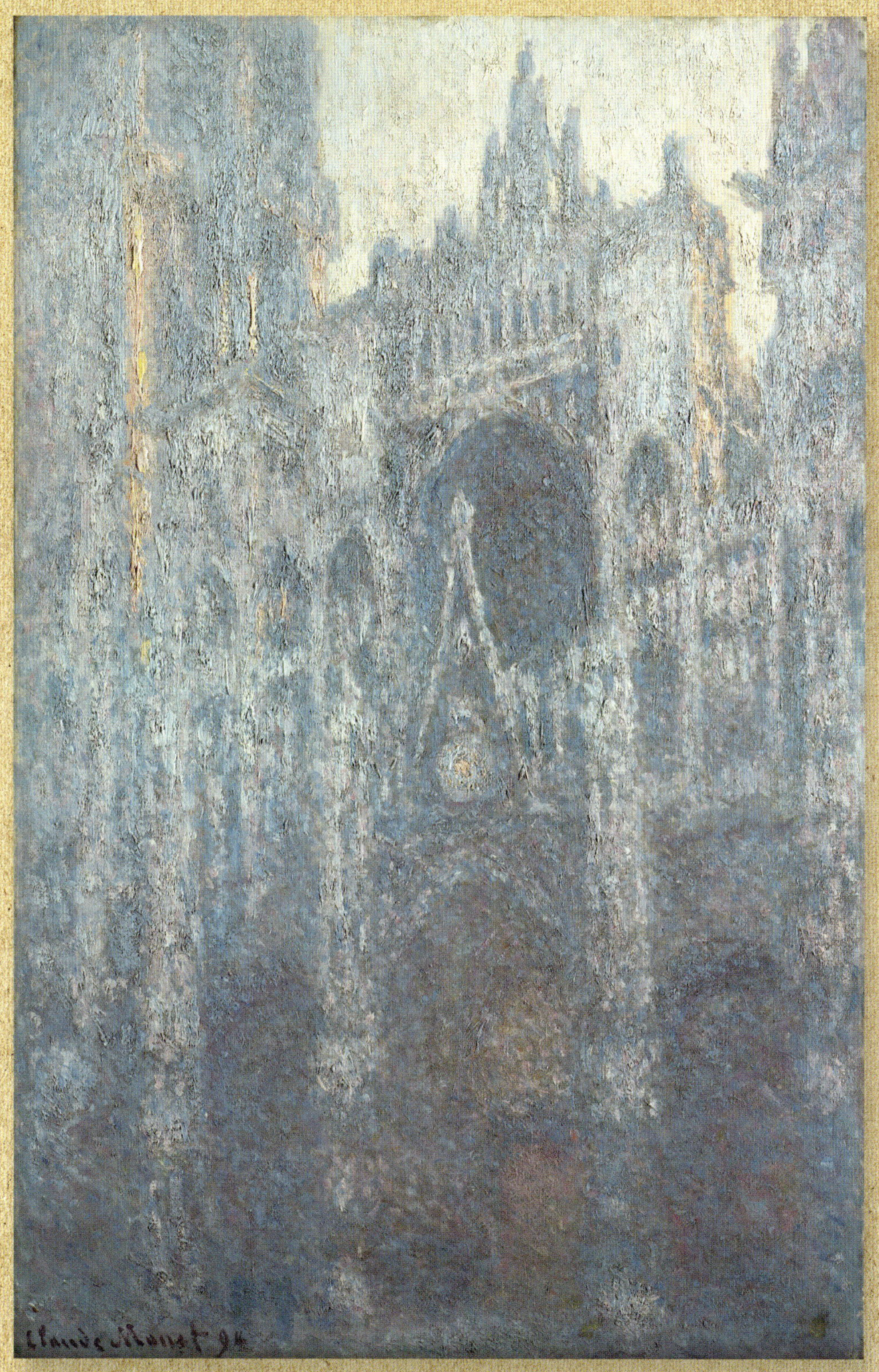

THE CARD PLAYERS
PAUL CÉZANNE (1839–1906)

the 30-second artwork

Cézanne was a leading painter
among the Post-Impressionists and a pivotal
figure in the future development of modern art.
In his work he moved away from naturalistic
depictions of colour and light, as found in the
work of the Impressionists, towards a focus on
the structure, form and abstract compositional
qualities of painting. *The Card Players* is part
of a series of works from the 1890s that have
become among the artist's most iconic paintings.
Along with numerous studies and sketches,
Cézanne completed five works in oil paint
depicting this theme, varying in size, number of
figures and the environment depicted. Although
he used local peasants from his hometown of
Aix-en-Provence as models for the paintings,
Cézanne was not aiming to capture a particular
scene of daily life. The focus is not on the
narrative of card playing but on the relationship
of mass, structure and colour. Each figure is
absorbed in contemplating their hand. They
do not interact with each other, and while there
is a bottle of wine on the table, there are no
glasses from which to drink its contents. The
pipe, playing cards and the men's shirt collars
add brighter elements that puncture the overall
warm tone of the picture.

DETAILS OF THE WORK
Oil on canvas, 1895
47.5 x 57 cm (18¾ x 22½ in)
Musée d'Orsay, Paris

3-SECOND BIOGRAPHY
PAULIN PAULET
Dates unknown
Paulet, a gardener on the
Cezanne family's estate Jas de
Bouffan, near Aix-en-Provence,
is thought to have posed for
the figure on the right in this
painting and in other versions
in the series

30-SECOND TEXT
Maria Alambritis

The textured, rough
facture of the paint
draws our attention
to the formal qualities
of the artwork.

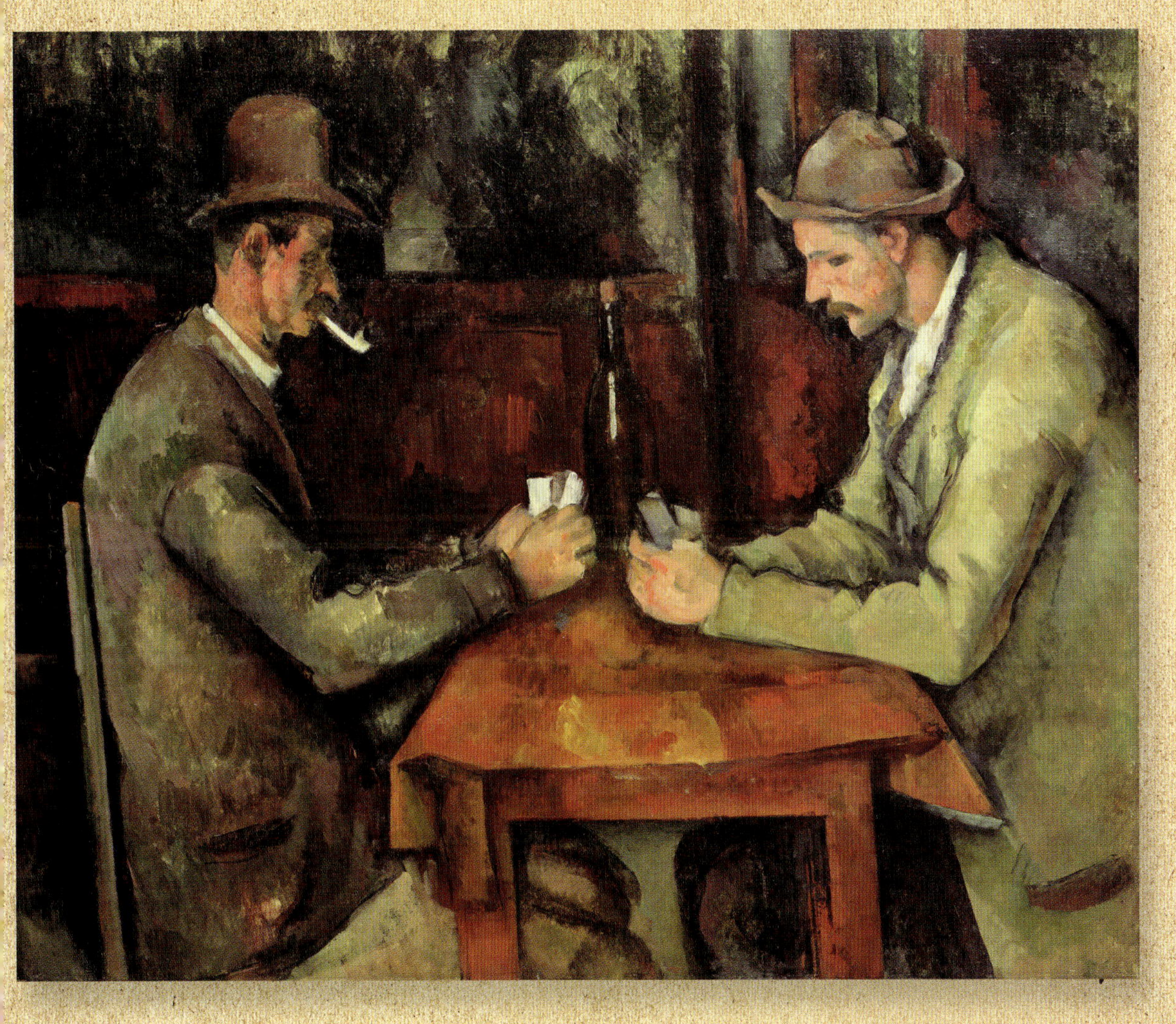

MODERNISM

abstract Abstract, as distinct from figurative art, does not aim to depict or copy the visual appearance of the external world. Although objects, people and things, may provide some form of inspiration for the artist, the artwork will not display any evidence of imitation.

aesthetic Criteria concerning the appreciation and judgement of beauty and taste in the visual arts.

Analytical Cubism Early innovative phase of Cubism developed by Picasso and Georges Braque around 1908. Rejecting the established conventions of perspective, they represented three-dimensional objects on a flat surface by depicting multiple viewpoints simultaneously as a series of complex, interwoven planes painted within a limited range of colours.

Art Nouveau International decorative style in architecture and design popular during the late nineteenth and early twentieth century. Taking inspiration from natural forms, it is typified by flowing lines and asymmetrical patterns.

collage The creation of an artwork by arranging and sticking fragments of printed and coloured paper or cloth developed by the Cubists. The possibility of incorporating image, language and form, as a means of creating ridiculous juxtapositions or to make political statements, made it popular with Dada and Surrealist artists.

Dada Avant-garde anti-art group that employed performance, poetry and radical forms of the visual arts to challenge accepted conventions in Western society. Emerging in Zurich during the First World War, before finding support in other European cities, the group was known for it provocative use of ridicule and nonsense.

De Stijl Influential abstract art movement arising from the magazine of the same name founded in 1917 by Mondrian and Theo van Doesburg in Holland. Meaning 'The Style' in Dutch, the group endorsed a pared-down geometric form of art employing a reduced palette of primary and non-colours.

direct carving The carving of stone, wood or such materials by hand with a hammer and chisel. As opposed to modelling and casting, many twentieth-century modern sculptors believed this to be a more immediate and expressive method of working that resulted in artworks that were more truthful to the material from which they were made.

Expressionism Early twentieth-century movement originating in Germany that rejected realism in favour of a subjective and intuitive approach to the creation of art and poetry. More generally the term is applied to art that is recognized as the result of an artist's emotional response to an external subject.

masonite Light thin hardboard made by pressure moulding steam-cooked wood fibres. Patented in America in the 1920s, it soon became a popular alternative to canvas among artists.

mural Large painting mounted or applied directly onto a wall or ceiling. During the twentieth century, modern murals were used to convey political messages.

Neoplasticism Form of abstract art conceived by Mondrian and advocated in the pages of *De Stijl*. Mondrian stated that art should be asymmetrical, and solely consist of vertical and horizontal lines, primary colours, and black and white.

pastoral An idealized or romantic representation of the countryside.

primitivism The move among modern artists to seek inspiration from the art and artefacts of non-western tribal cultures, such as those of sub-Saharan Africa, South America and the Pacific islands, which they perceived as providing more authentic or genuine forms of expression. European folk art, and the art of children and psychiatric patients were also valued for their naivety and unsophistication.

psychoanalysis Theories and therapeutic technique devised by Sigmund Freud (1856–1939) that claimed patients could be cured of many conditions by the release and acknowledgement of repressed emotions and thoughts. Artists were particularly interested in its ideas relating to the unlocking of the unconscious mind and dream analysis.

Salon d'Automne Annual art exhibition held in Paris. Founded in 1903 by a group of artists and poets as an alternative to the official Salon, during its early years it held important retrospective exhibitions of the painters Gauguin and Cezanne.

Synthetic Cubism Secondary phase of Cubism, dating around 1912–14, notable for the development of collage incorporating newspaper, coloured paper and fabric. Paintings were likewise based on the arrangement of flat planes, text and pattern.

the 30-second artwork

Le bonheur de vivre (The Joy of Life) is a large painting depicting an idealized pastoral scene in brilliant, vibrant colours. It shows a forest clearing encircled by overhanging trees, opening out to the sea and the distant horizon. Nude figures are arranged about the scene, engaged in languorous, sensual pleasures, in harmony with nature. In the centre of the canvas a group is dancing in a circle with carefree abandon, emphasizing the fluid, circular nature of the composition. The figures are picked out and placed like separate elements or motifs in a decorative pattern. Matisse's intention is not to capture a realistic image from nature or an impression of light but to appeal to the viewer's senses, evoking an emotional response through colour and pattern. Matisse originally studied law but took up art during a period of ill health, and a subsequent apprenticeship gave him a grounding in traditional painting techniques. His work changed dramatically when, inspired by the brilliant light of the South of France, he developed the characteristic qualities seen in this painting. This new work represented a radical break from tradition and was initially derided as wild and primitive, but Matisse came to be regarded, alongside Picasso, as one of the defining artists of the early twentieth century.

3-SECOND SKETCH

Matisse's paintings are characterized by bold colours and a sense of joyous hedonism. Their sensual, decorative qualities reflect his interest in eastern art and textiles.

3-MINUTE STUDY

Les Fauves ('the wild beasts') was a term coined by the critic Louis Vauxcelles to describe the paintings of Matisse and a group of associated artists exhibited at the Salon d'Automne in 1905. Fauvism emphasized individual expression and highlighted colour as an independent element within a painting, separate from its representative, figurative purpose. The simplified forms and flat planes of different colours make Fauvism a significant precursor to Cubism and later abstractionist movements.

DETAILS OF THE WORK

Oil on canvas, 1905–6
176.5 x 240.7 cm (69½ x 94¾ in)
Barnes Foundation, Philadelphia

3-SECOND BIOGRAPHY

GUSTAVE MOREAU
1826–98
French Symbolist painter and early influence on Matisse, particularly in the emphasis he placed on personal expression

30-SECOND TEXT

Paul Harper

This massive canvas is regarded as one of the pillars of Modernist painting.

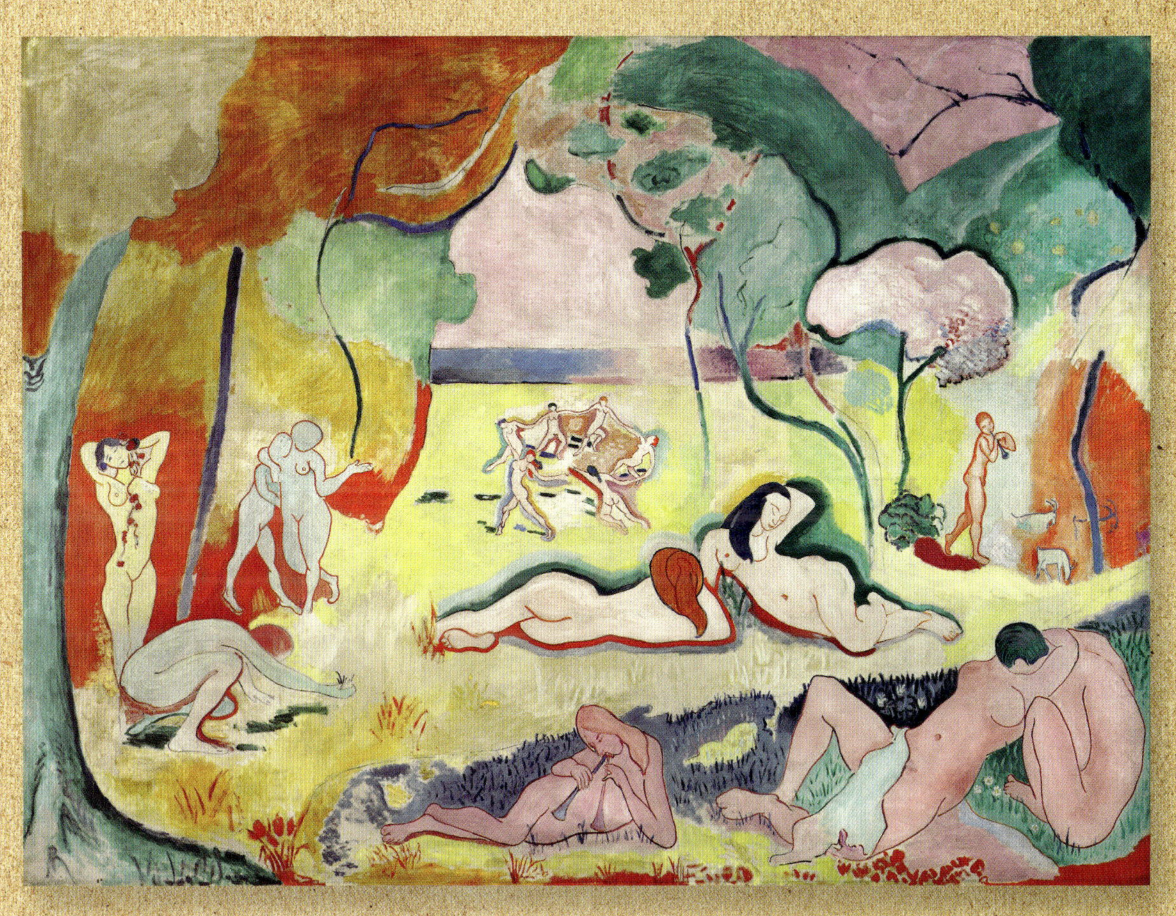

the 30-second artwork

This huge canvas, almost four metres square, shows two lovers locked together in a passionate embrace. They are dressed in luxuriously ornamented and symbolically contrasting gowns. The impression is of two people losing themselves in swooning ecstasy. The flowery meadow on which they stand, the night sky behind them and the golden cloth that enfolds the lovers are barely representational, forming a dreamlike, richly decorative, almost abstract composition. Early in his career Klimt had achieved some recognition as a conventional academic painter but in developing the distinctive personal style that is evident in this work he embraced the modern movements that were influencing European art at the time, as well as drawing on styles from Japanese, Byzantine and Egyptian art. He combined naturalistic imagery with stylized forms and decorative abstraction, often imbuing his work with an atmosphere of allegory and symbolism. Although he painted landscapes and portraits, the female body was a frequent motif in his work, characterized by an overt, languid sensuality. Through his combined use of sinuous, organic and stylized geometric forms he became one of the most influential exponents of the Art Nouveau movement, which in his native Austria was known as Jugendstil.

3-SECOND SKETCH
A leading cultural figure in decadent Vienna at the beginning of the twentieth century, Klimt combined stylized and naturalistic forms in flattened, richly decorative images.

3-MINUTE STUDY
Klimt was associated with the Wiener Werkstätte, a workshop that was one of the early incarnations of European Modernism, founded to improve standards of design and manufacture, and to elevate everyday objects to the status of fine art. While some of Klimt's Modernist contemporaries, such as Adolf Loos, were opposed to decoration, he sought to create a *Gesamtkunstwerk* or total work of art, a union of the visual arts, expressly through the use of ornament.

DETAILS OF THE WORK
Oil and gold leaf on canvas, 1907–8
180 x 180 cm (70¾ x 70¾ in)
Belvedere Museum, Vienna

3-SECOND BIOGRAPHY
EGON SCHIELE
1890–1918
A protégé of Klimt's and a major figure in Austrian Expressionist painting, whose emotionally intense, erotic images were greatly influenced by the older artist

30-SECOND TEXT
Paul Harper

*With its extensively gilded surface, **The Kiss** represents the highpoint of Klimt's 'Golden Period'.*

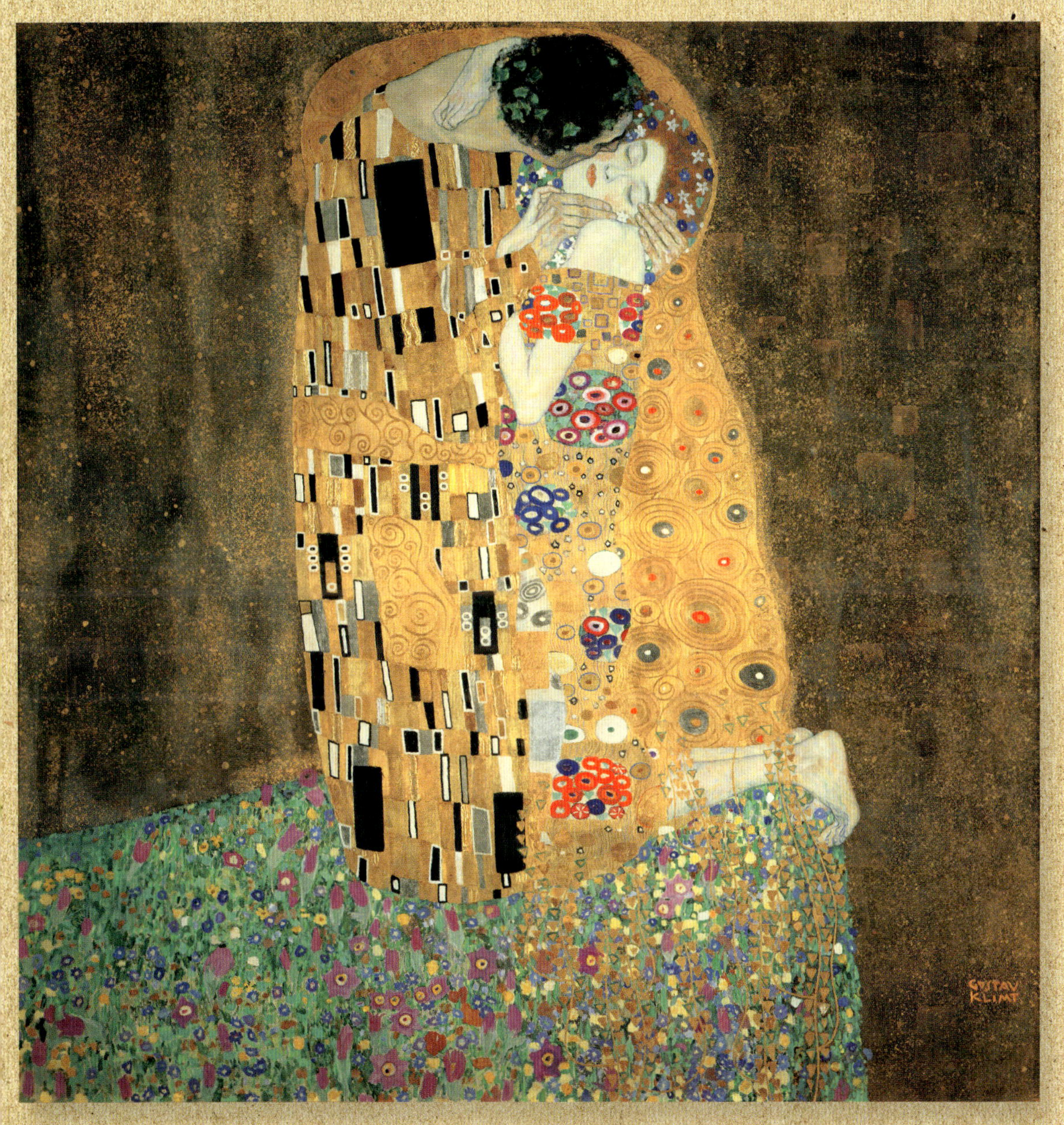

the 30-second artwork

This bronze sculpture shows a figure, caught in a transitional state between human and machine, striding forward with heroic determination. The muscular, dynamic compulsion of the form is emphasized by distortions suggesting wind and speed. While Boccioni's early works were in an Impressionist style, in 1910 he became one of the principal artists and theorists of the Italian Futurist group, for whom he wrote a number of essays setting out his ideas on the relationship between form, space and motion. *Unique Forms* perfectly embodies the Futurist celebration of the energy and transformative possibilities of modernity. He believed that a central task for the artist was to represent the experience of movement, which he saw as a defining characteristic of the modern condition. The sense of arrested flow and the deconstruction of the body into overlapping planes and geometric shapes are qualities reminiscent of Analytical Cubism, an important influence on Boccioni's visual language. The Futurists romanticized the violently regenerative potential of conflict, and Boccioni campaigned for Italy to enter the First World War. He died while volunteering in the Italian Army at the age of 33. During Boccioni's lifetime this work existed only as a plaster version. It was finally cast in bronze in 1931.

3-SECOND SKETCH
Capturing movement developing in time and space, *Unique Forms* expresses Futurist preoccupations with speed and the transformation of human experience in a mechanized future.

3-MINUTE STUDY
Boccioni is considered to be Futurism's leading art theorist and was hugely influential in shaping its aesthetic principles. He believed that other Modernists were stuck in what he termed 'analytical discontinuity', arguing that the Cubists lacked vitality and had failed to capture life in the round. In his sculpture he sought to achieve 'synthetic continuity'. Instead of simply representing action, he endeavoured to capture essential truths about motion through expressive abstraction.

DETAILS OF THE WORK
Plaster, 1913; bronze, 1931
111 x 88 cm (43¾ x 34¾ in)
Various

3-SECOND BIOGRAPHY
FILIPPO TOMMASO EMILIO MARINETTI
1876–1944
Poet and writer who, in 1909, published the first Futurist Manifesto, an aggressive rejection of the past and a romanticized vision of the industrialized world

30-SECOND TEXT
Paul Harper

In this work Boccioni captures what he called 'synthetic continuity', the rushing fluidity of action.

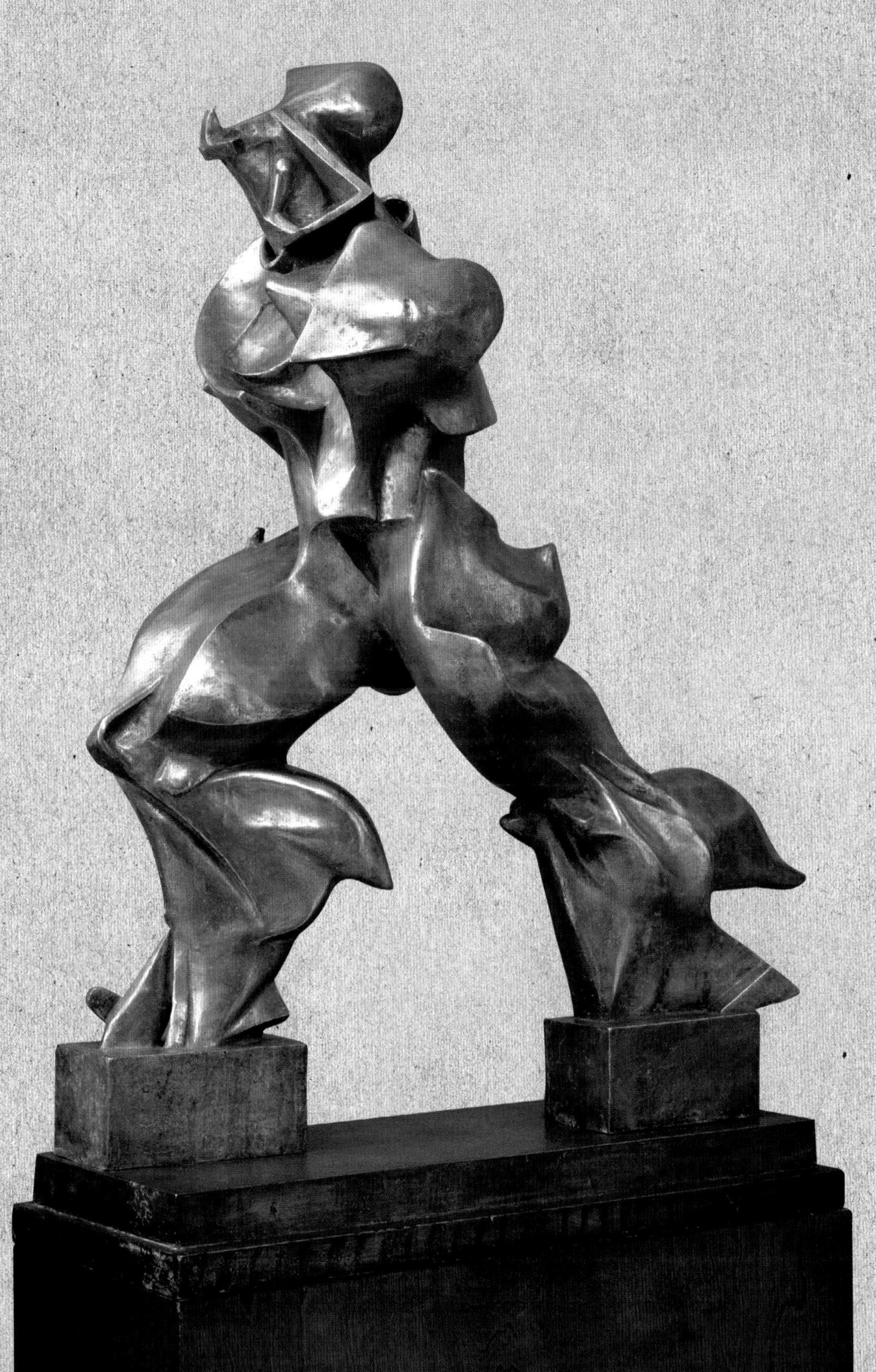

THE TREACHERY OF IMAGES
RENÉ MAGRITTE (1898–1967)

the 30-second artwork

Below a simple, graphic rendering of a pipe is written in French, *'Ceci n'est pas une pipe.'* or 'This is not a pipe.' Text and image are placed together to make an apparent paradox. Of course, neither the visual representation of the pipe nor the word 'pipe' is an actual pipe. The apparent banality of the painting and the statement belies the complex interaction of image, text and the thing itself. Probably the best-known Belgian artist of the twentieth century, Magritte is closely associated with Surrealism. *The Treachery of Images* belongs to a series from the 1920s that used devices such as contradictory statements, the misnaming of objects and dreamlike juxtapositions to question conventions of knowledge and representation and the uncanny transaction between subjectivity and objectivity in our reading of the world. Surrealist in nature, his paintings can also be seen as rational attempts to understand the relationship between modes of representation and reality. Stylistically, they have a concrete, illustrative quality, evoking the commercial art by which he earned his living for many years – producing advertising and book designs. This deadpan, apparently conservative, aesthetic amplifies the sense of mystery, the dreamlike strangeness and the disconcerting, sometimes violent incongruities in his work.

The Treachery of Images *wittily undermines the accepted relationship between image, text and object.*

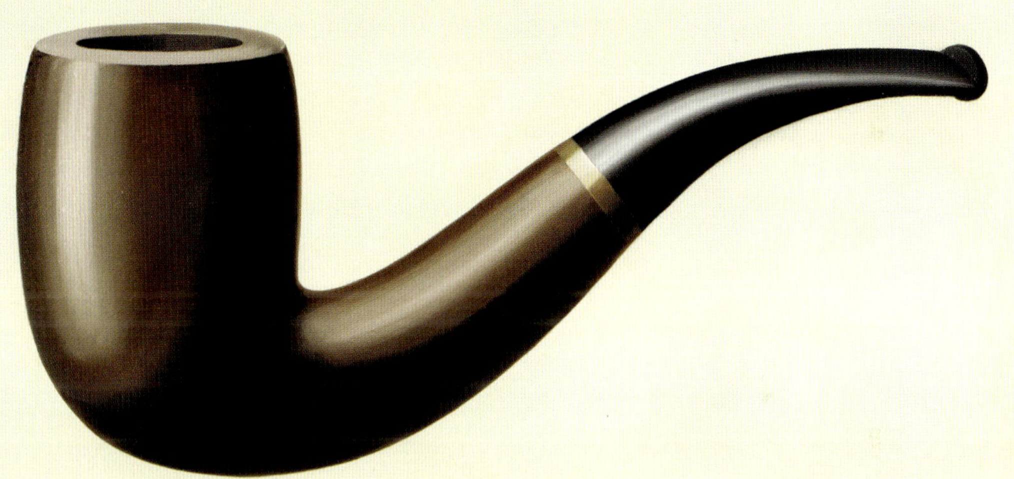
Ceci n'est pas une pipe.
Magritte

COMPOSITION A WITH RED AND BLUE
PIET MONDRIAN (1872–1945)

the 30-second artwork

A simple asymmetrical grid

structure, delineated by black lines, contains two blocks of flat, primary colour, separated by blocks of white. The comparative scale and arrangement of the two colours within the grid creates a balanced sense of harmony and energy. Mondrian had experimented with the principles of Analytical Cubism: analyzing objects into planes of simple form and shade composed in the flat space of the painting. Mondrian continued to simplify this approach, developing an aesthetic language that he felt could represent the whole range of visual experience in a manner that was abstract and universal. This style, which he called Neoplasticism, consisted of square or rectangular forms, defined by straight horizontal and vertical black lines, and a limited palate of grey, white and the primary colours. Mondrian's simple formula could be arranged in an infinitely variable set of relationships, with all the elements held in dynamic balance. It embodied a utopian ideal of spiritual coherence. The anonymous beauty of this idiom, reduced to the essentials of form and colour, expressed both the rational principles of International Modernism and its aspiration that a work of art should be autonomous, rather than an illusion of the external visual world.

3-SECOND SKETCH
The asymmetrical balance and simplified visual language of this painting, devoid of any reference to the outside world, perfectly expresses Mondrian's aspiration towards pure abstraction.

3-MINUTE STUDY
Mondrian co-founded the Dutch artistic movement De Stijl with Theo van Doesburg (1883–1931). De Stijl, which translates as 'The Style', was originally a publication in which Mondrian wrote a series of articles setting out his ideas on aesthetics. De Stijl had a profound influence on the development of abstract art and modern architecture and design. Mondrian later withdrew from De Stijl, having fallen out with van Doesburg over the introduction of diagonal elements into his work.

DETAILS OF THE WORK
Oil on canvas, 1932
55.5 x 55.5 cm (22 x 22 in)
Kunstmuseum, Winterthur

3-SECOND BIOGRAPHY
GERRIT RIETVELD
1888–1964
Furniture designer and architect and a principal member of De Stijl; influenced by Mondrian, as can be seen in Rietveld's *Red and Blue Chair*

30-SECOND TEXT
Paul Harper

Composition A with Red and Blue *embodies Mondrian's ideal of spiritual harmony and order.*

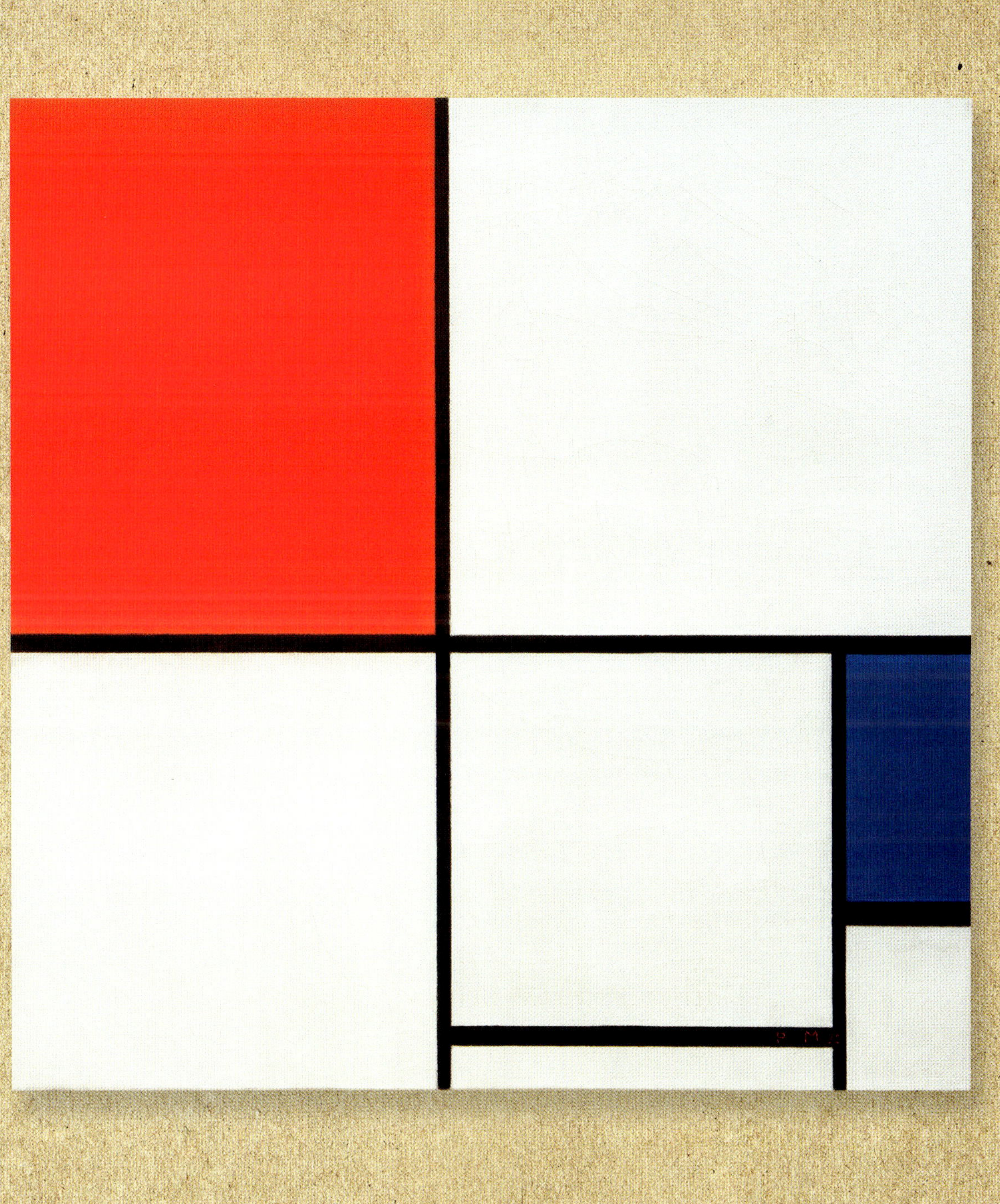

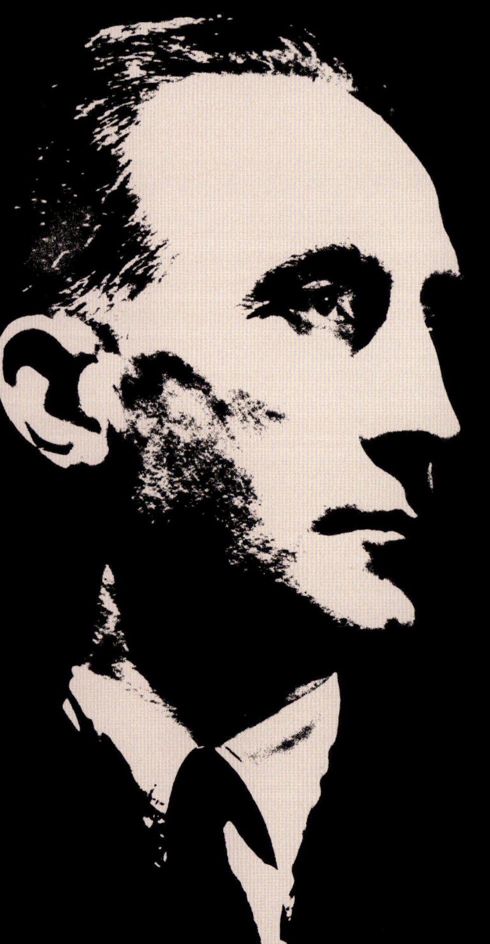

1887
Born in Blainville-Crevon, Normandy in Northern France on 28 July

1904
Studies art at the Académie Julian in Paris

1908
Exhibits at the prestigious Salon d'Automne

1913
Nude Descending a Staircase, No.2 exhibited at the New York Armory Show

1913
Duchamp makes the first 'readymade', a bicycle wheel mounted on a stool

1917
Fountain is exhibited in New York

1921
The periodical *New York Dada* is published by Duchamp and Man Ray

1927
The Bride Stripped Bare by her Bachelors, Even (The Large Glass) shown at the International Exhibition of Modern Art at the Brooklyn Museum in 1927

1966
Completes his final artwork, *Étant donnés: 1° la chute d'eau / 2° le gaz d'éclairage*

1968
Dies at home in Neuilly-sur-Seine, France on 2 October

2004
Fountain named as the most influential artwork of the twentieth century in a survey of 500 renowned artists and art historians

MARCEL DUCHAMP

Marcel Duchamp can be seen as the single most influential artist of the twentieth century, disrupting almost every established convention about what art should be and how it should be made.

In his early career Duchamp had found some success as a painter, but, having encountered the Dada movement, he declared that he was no longer interested in what he called 'retinal art' – art intended to please the eye. Seeking an alternative to representation or illusion in art, he began to exhibit commonplace objects that he called 'readymades', often choosing mass-produced, utilitarian items. This emphasis on the process of selection, rather than creation, fundamentally undermined accepted views regarding the role of the artist.

The readymade also challenged the notion that art should be beautiful. Duchamp said that he selected everyday objects precisely because of their lack of visual distinction. Their value had nothing to do with bourgeois notions of good or bad taste, instead residing in how effectively they could embody an idea. In this regard, Duchamp could be seen as having laid the foundations of Conceptual Art – art that valued ideas over formal or visual qualities.

In 1917 Duchamp called the bluff of the Society of Independent Artists in New York, which, at his suggestion, had advertised a jury-free exhibition open to work of every kind. Taking them at their word, Duchamp submitted a ready-made porcelain urinal, signed 'R. Mutt' and titled *Fountain*. This was duly refused entry, as the artist had possibly intended. His point had been to argue that what mattered was not who had made the object but rather the fact that he, Duchamp, had chosen it – designating it as 'art'.

His argument was consistent with the trajectory established by Cubism and abstract art, which had abandoned the notion of truth to nature as a criterion for judging painting and sculpture. If art was no longer to be valued in terms of its life-likeness, and thus of the traditional skills associated with painting or sculpting, then perhaps the distinction between art and non-art lay not in how things looked or were made, but in how successful the art object was in stimulating discussion.

While Duchamp's eclectic use of materials contributed to the diversification of sculptural practice in the twentieth century, his foregrounding of theoretical and conceptual issues in the making and presentation of an artwork continues to resonate throughout the art world to this day.

Paul Harper

the 30-second artwork

Weeping Woman is a compelling representation of inconsolable grief. A sobbing woman holds a handkerchief to her face. The central area of the painting, corresponding to the handkerchief, is picked out in monochrome, framed in stark contrast by vivid colours. This contrast shapes the composition and seems to emphasize the intensity of feeling. *Weeping Woman* is one of a series of paintings made in the course of 1937 that relate to the epic painting *Guernica*. But where *Guernica* depicted the horrors of a particular event in the Spanish Civil War, with these other, smaller works Picasso was trying to create a universal image of human suffering. He drew on baroque sculptures of the weeping Virgin, a figure often depicted in exuberantly sentimental and pious detail. This kind of reference to art-historical precedents is typical of his work. Picasso is regarded as one of the most original artists of the twentieth century. Together with Georges Braque he invented Cubism, but he also pioneered the use of collage and was closely associated with diverse movements such as Symbolism and Surrealism. He was extraordinarily prolific and, although he saw himself primarily as a painter, he was also a hugely influential sculptor and made significant experiments in a range of other media such as printmaking and ceramics.

3-SECOND SKETCH
The subject's face is rationalized into overlapping and fragmented planes and viewpoints, deconstructing the traditional conventions of perspective. This is characteristic of Picasso's Analytical Cubism.

3-MINUTE STUDY
Responding to the bombing of the Basque town of Guernica by the German Luftwaffe in support of General Franco's Nationalist forces, Picasso created the vast painting *Guernica*. Over the following year he made a series of studies based on one of the figures in the painting – a woman holding her dead child. *Weeping Woman* is the last and most fully realized of the series. The figure is based on Picasso's then lover, Dora Maar.

DETAILS OF THE WORK
Oil on canvas, 1937
60 x 49 cm (23½ x 19¼ in)
Tate Modern, London

3-SECOND BIOGRAPHY
GEORGES BRAQUE
1882–1963
Collaborated with Picasso to develop Cubism in first its Analytical and then its Synthetic forms

30-SECOND TEXT
Paul Harper

Weeping Woman *is a powerful study of human suffering, intensified by Picasso's fragmentary Cubist technique.*

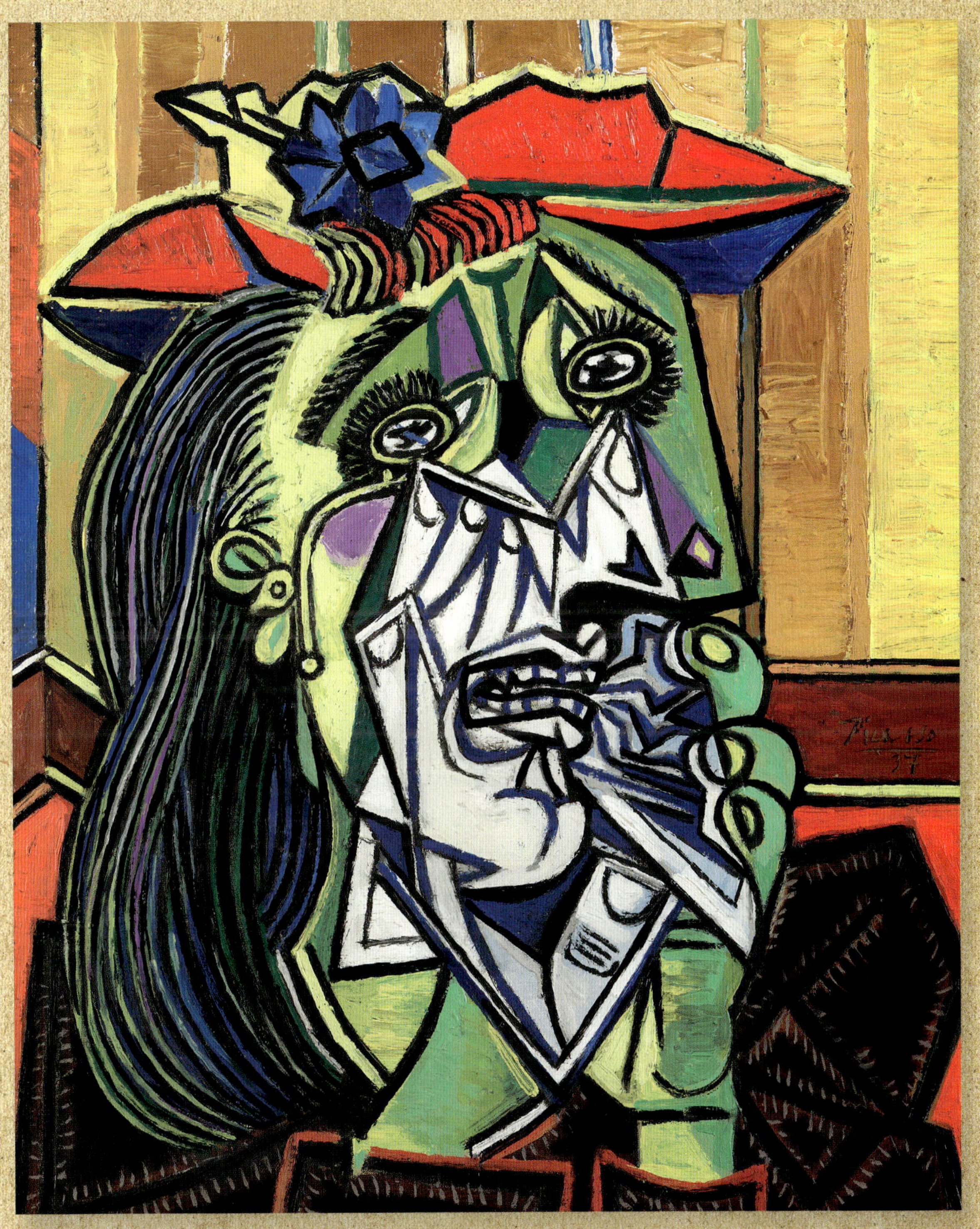

WAVE
DAME BARBARA HEPWORTH
(1903–75)

the 30-second artwork

Inspired by the landscape of

Cornwall, where Hepworth had been living since 1939, *Wave* is typical of the work that she was making at this time. Although the sculpture is abstract, it powerfully evokes landscape and natural forms. The smooth oval shape partially contains a void. There is a tension between the mass of the form and the absence that it encompasses, emphasized by the contrast between the polished exterior and the painted interior. This tension is further dramatized by the play of light and shadow, and by nylon strings stretched in a radiating pattern across the void. The experience of being in the landscape was an important factor in shaping Hepworth's approach to sculpture, along with the inherent characteristics of her chosen materials and the carving process itself. Having combined figurative and abstract forms in her early career, her work became increasingly less representational until it reached a point of almost complete abstraction. However, nature and landscape were always present in her art, which can be seen as being primarily about relationships: between the interior and exterior of objects; between colour and texture; between objects placed together; between the human figure and the landscape; and between sculpture and the landscape.

DETAILS OF THE WORK
Wood, paint, string, 1943
30.5 x 44.5 x 21 cm (12 x 17½ x 8¼ in)
SNGMA, Edinburgh

3-SECOND BIOGRAPHY
BEN NICHOLSON
1894–1982
English artist and pioneering exponent of abstract art; married to Hepworth from 1938 to 1951

30-SECOND TEXT
Paul Harper

Wave explores the dynamic interplay between the exterior mass and interior space of an object.

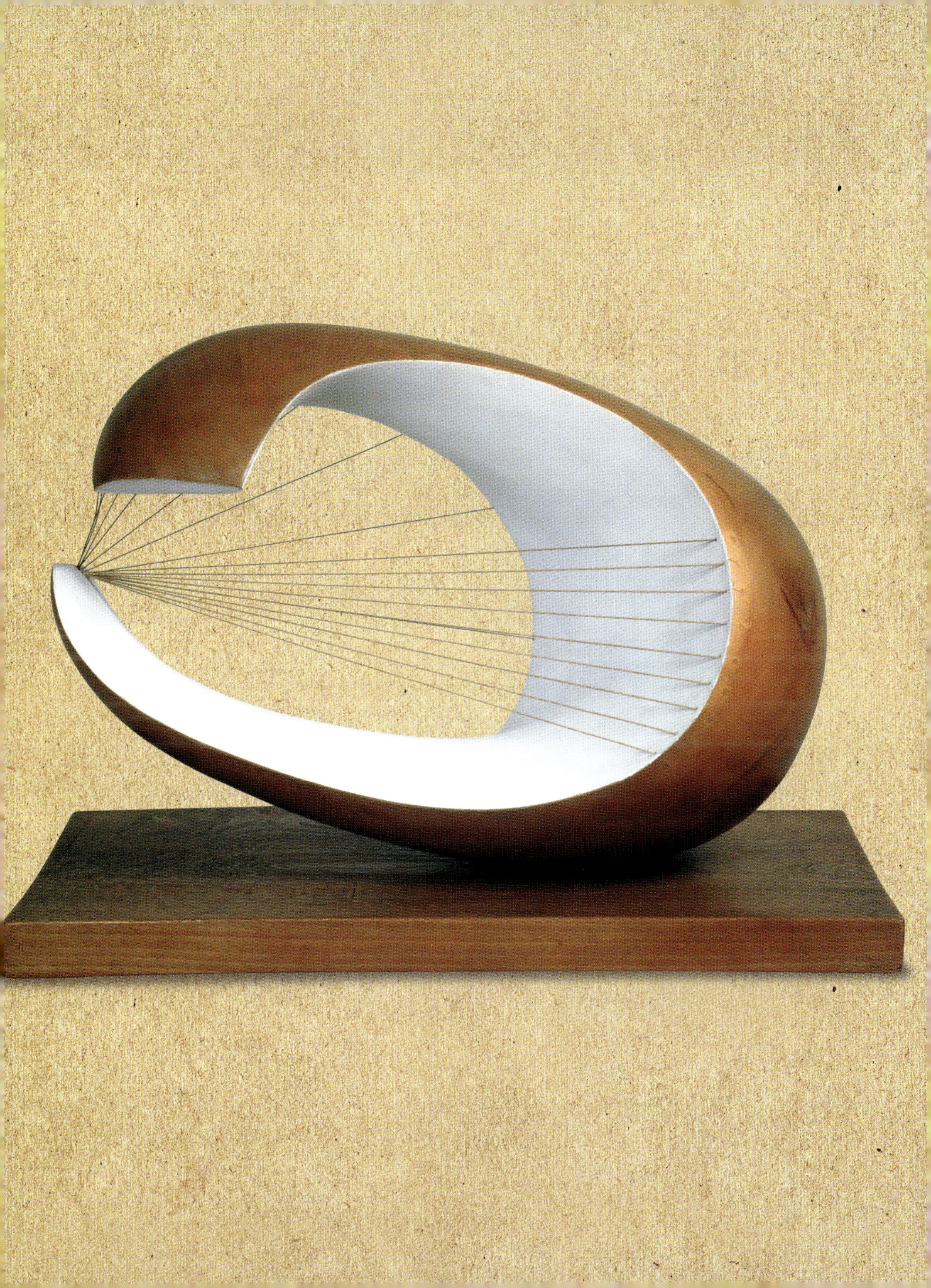

SELF-PORTRAIT AS A TEHUANA, OR DIEGO ON MY MIND

FRIDA KAHLO (1907–54)

the 30-second artwork

In this self-portrait Kahlo is dressed in traditional Mexican 'Tehuana' costume. Typically, the work is autobiographical. Across her brow she has painted a portrait of her husband, the artist Diego Rivera, with whom she had a volatile relationship. Radiating out from an elaborate headdress formed of plants surrounded by lace is a network of threads, suggesting an organic network of roots or nerve endings. She stares out from the painting with a direct look that is at once tragic, dignified and confrontational. In her childhood Kahlo had suffered with polio and then as a young adult she was involved in a traumatic bus crash that left her with multiple injuries. For most of her life she was in terrible pain. The physical and psychological legacy of these experiences was a major influence on her work, along with her troubled, obsessive love for the unfaithful Rivera, her socialism and her fascination with Mexican folk art and national identity. With her rich symbolic visual language, psychological intensity and fantastical elements, Kahlo has been linked to the Surrealists, and her work was shown in a major Surrealist exhibition in Mexico in 1940. However, she rejected the label, insisting that her paintings are directly autobiographical, depicting her own, concrete reality rather than the revealed products of her subconscious.

DETAILS OF THE WORK
Oil on masonite, 1943
76 x 61 cm (30 x 24 in)
Jacques and Natasha Gelman Collection, Mexico City

3-SECOND BIOGRAPHY
DIEGO RIVERA
1886–1957
Regarded as the most important Mexican artist of the twentieth century, famous for his large, politically charged murals

30-SECOND TEXT
Paul Harper

Kahlo resolutely meets the viewer's gaze and proudly displays her passion for Rivera.

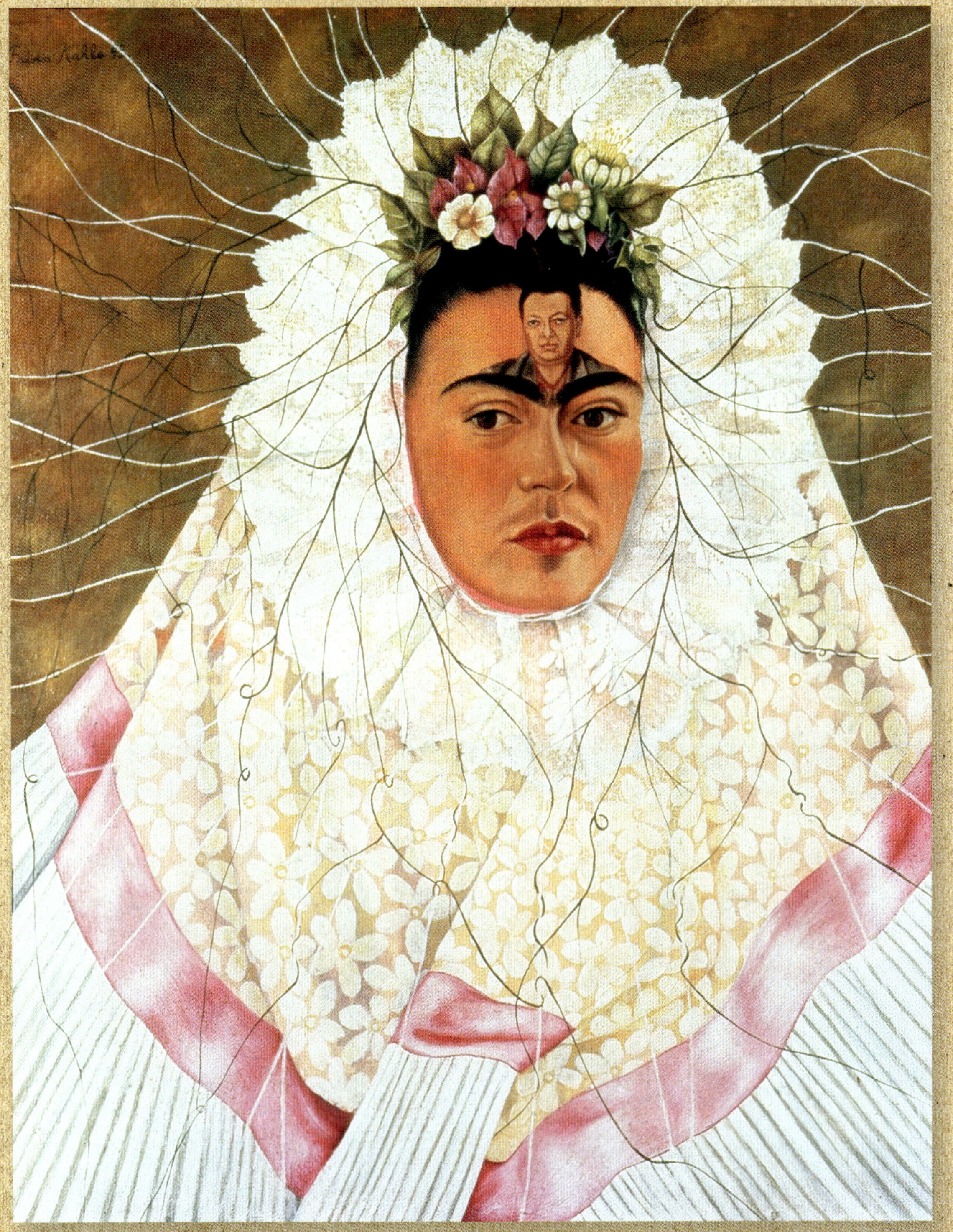

POST-WAR TO TODAY

Abstract Expressionism American art movement arising in the decades that followed the Second World War. Artists associated with the group were known for painting large, predominantly non-figurative canvases.

Action Painting Expressive, gestural form of abstract art in which paint is often spontaneously thrown, dripped or rubbed onto a canvas or board. Epitomized by the work of Jackson Pollock.

assemblage The bringing together and arrangement of traditionally non-art materials and found objects to form an artwork. Pioneered by Cubist, Dada and Surrealist artists, this is a method that continues to be explored in contemporary art today.

Colour Field Type of post-war abstract painting that prioritized the use of colour as a form of expression. The preference for flat saturated expanses of paint places it in contrast to the bold gestural marks of Action Painting.

Conceptual Art Artwork in which the concept, or idea, is more important than the work as an image or object. Usually avoiding explicit signs of craftsmanship, it can appear in many forms including text, photography, film and sound.

encaustic Ancient painting technique that mixes coloured pigment with hot wax. On setting, the wax acts as a binder for the pigment.

facsimile An exact copy of text or image.

formalism Critical assessment of art that focuses on an artwork's form – for example, colour, line, texture or technique – rather than its subject or the social or historical context of its making.

monumental Applied to a large and often imposing sculpture. These qualities give the artwork an appearance of importance and permanence.

Op Art (Optical Art) Abstract art movement emerging in the 1960s that experimented with the optical effects of line, form and colour. Employing repetitive patterns or designs, the static surfaces of the large canvases can appear to undulate and pulsate.

pedestal The base on which a statue or other three-dimensional artwork sits. In the twentieth century many artists began to create sculptures that abandoned the pedestal in order to bring the artwork closer to the viewer.

picture plane The imaginary plane represented by the surface of a painting or drawing. In the Western tradition in art it has been thought of as a hypothetical window through which the viewer sees the imaginary scene beyond. This is one of the many conventions challenged by modern artists through their emphasis on the physicality of the artwork.

plywood Widely used commercial board. It is manufactured by gluing together multiple layers of thin wood veneer with the grain of each layer rotated to create strength. It was first used by artists as an alternative to canvas or panel in the late nineteenth century.

Pointillism A technique pioneered by the nineteenth-century French artists Georges Seurat and Paul Signac that created images using distinct small dots of pure colour. When seen from a relative distance these colours blend together in the eye of the viewer to create a greater tonal range.

Pop Art Far-reaching art movement that appeared concurrently in Britain and the USA in the 1950s, influenced by the bold graphics and striking designs of post-war popular culture. Rejecting the conventional methods and motifs of high art, they looked for inspiration among comic books, product packaging and advertisements.

Postmodernism An overarching term that is applied to a diverse range of artistic practice from the 1960s onwards that is opposed to the twentieth-century dominance of Modernism and its shaping principles of idealism and universal truth. Postmodern art often favours uncertainty, contradiction and the blurring of boundaries regarding the conventions of art.

silkscreen printing A form of printmaking in which multiple layers of colour are built up by squeezing paint or ink through a fine silk screen. Masking sections of the silk prevents areas of a specific colour passing through to create a design.

Venice Biennale International contemporary art exhibition held in Venice every two years. Founded in 1895, the biennale has become one of the art world's most respected events and attracts artists from across the globe.

ALCHEMY
JACKSON POLLOCK (1912–56)

the 30-second artwork

In 1947 Pollock abandoned his Surrealist-inspired paintings and pioneered a radical new form of abstract art. Rejecting brush and easel, he spread his canvas on the floor and began pouring paint straight from the tin. Using a stick to gain more control, he dripped, flicked and splattered his paintings from all angles. The resulting images appear haphazard, but Pollock maintained that nothing was left to chance; though the flow of paint was spontaneous, he claimed to be guided by intuition and emotion. 'Action Painting' was the term that art critic Harold Rosenberg used to describe Pollock's energetic new style, of which *Alchemy* is a prime example. With no discernible focal point, every part of the image is of equal importance. While this confused some viewers when the paintings were first exhibited in 1948 at the Betty Parsons Gallery, others were quick to praise the work. The influential critic Clement Greenberg described Pollock as the greatest American painter of the twentieth century, and Pollock soon found himself at the centre of a new movement in art – Abstract Expressionism – with fellow artists Barnett Newman and Willem de Kooning. By the mid-1950s he had become the best-known artist in America, if not the world, before in 1956 a fatal car crash cut short his burgeoning career.

3-SECOND SKETCH
This chaotic tangle of dribbled lines and splashes of colour is an early example of the infamous drip technique which helped propel Pollock to international fame.

3-MINUTE STUDY
Interpretations of this painting have often relied on its evocative title, which originated not with Pollock but with his friend and neighbour, Ralph Manheim. Pollock later worried that such titles encouraged viewers to look for predetermined meanings in his paintings rather than taking them at face value as he intended. Believing that his work should be free from all references to the external world, he later abandoned titling his paintings and started numbering them instead.

DETAILS OF THE WORK
Oil on fabric, 1947
114.6 x 221.3 cm (45⅛ x 87⅛ in)
Guggenheim Collection, Venice

3-SECOND BIOGRAPHIES
BETTY PARSONS
1900–82
Artist and gallery owner who championed Pollock's radical new style of painting

HAROLD ROSENBERG
1906–78
American art critic who coined the term 'Action Painting'

30-SECOND TEXT
David Trigg

Pollock's new painting technique baffled many, but he was soon acknowledged as the leading artist of his generation.

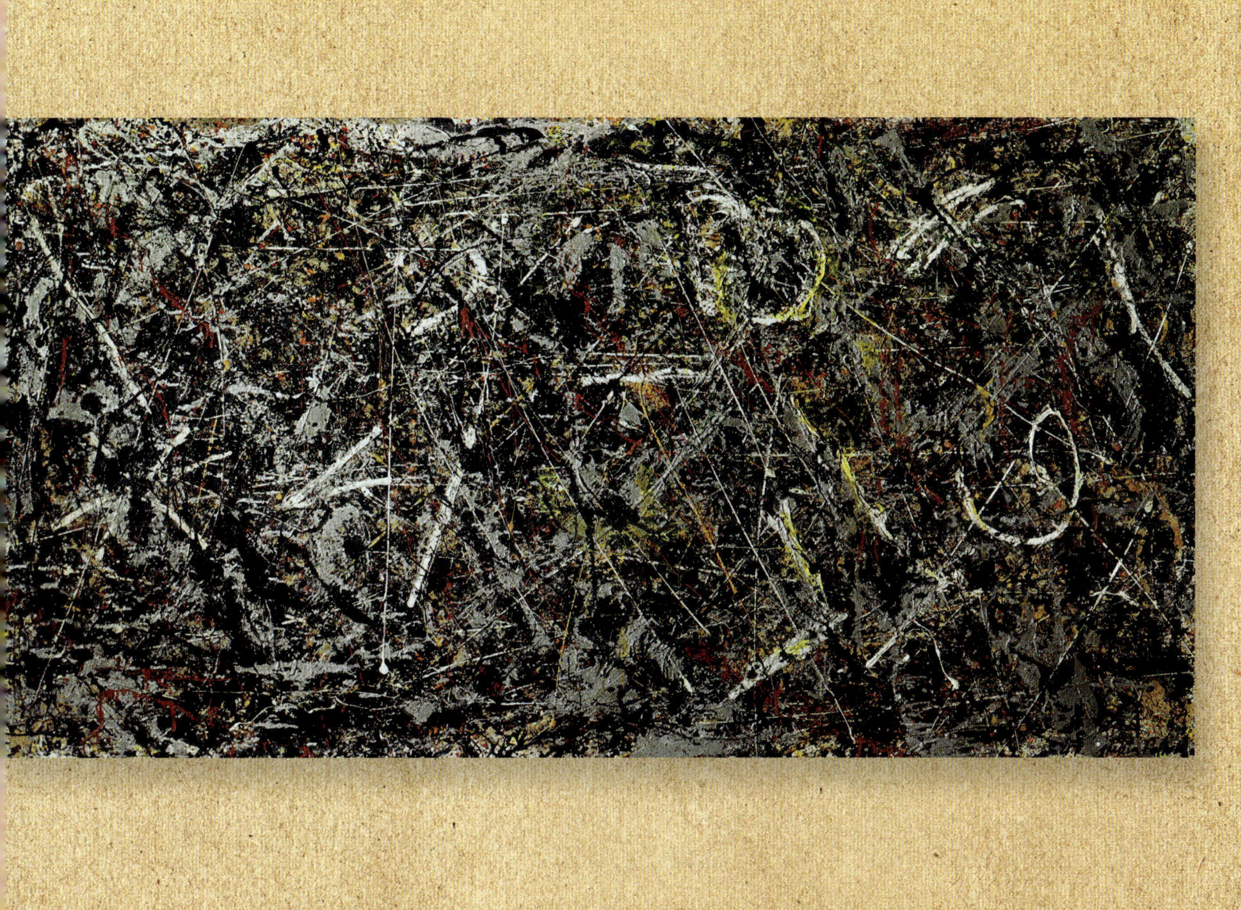

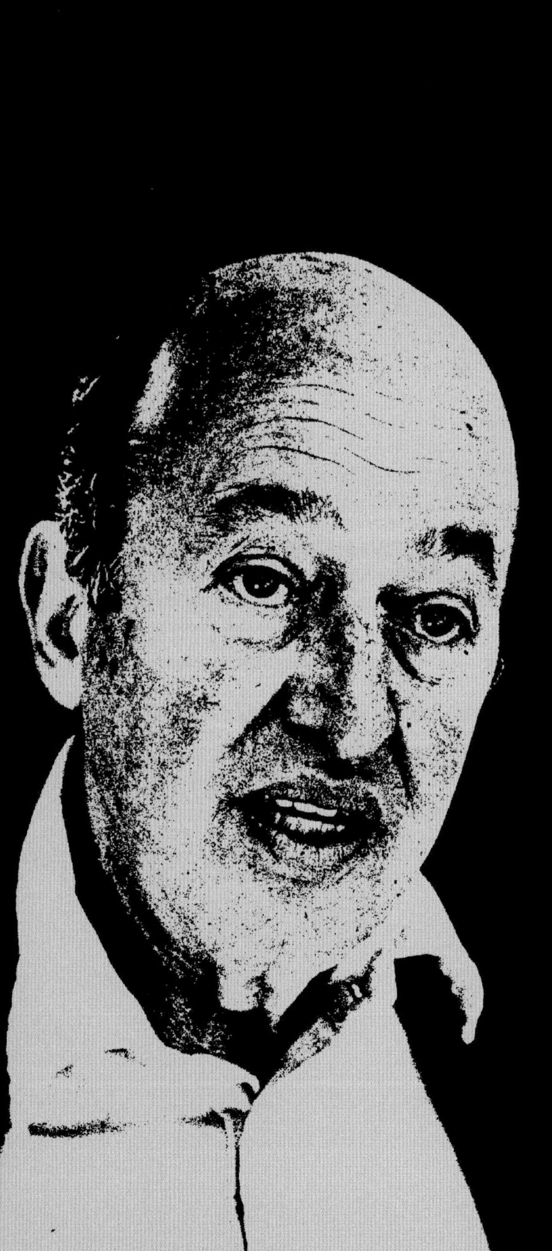

1909
Born in the Bronx, New York City, on 16 January

1930
Graduates from Syracuse University with a degree in English Literature

1937
Begins to write seriously, publishing art criticism in small magazines and literary journals

1939
Publishes the influential essay 'Avant-Garde and Kitsch' in *Partisan Review*

1942
Appointed art critic for the left-wing journal the *Nation* (1942–49)

1955
Writes 'American-Type Painting', one of his central statements about the development of modern art

1960
Writes 'Modernist Painting', an important essay explaining his aesthetic viewpoint

1961
Art and Culture, an anthology of Greenberg's essays, is published

1964
Curates the Post-Painterly Abstraction exhibition at the Los Angeles County Museum of Art

1994
Dies in New York City on 7 May

CLEMENT GREENBERG

Clement Greenberg was one of the best-known art critics of the twentieth century. His writings on art have influenced generations of artists, critics and historians. He was most closely associated with the American Abstract Expressionist movement and was the first to champion the work of Jackson Pollock. He was an advisor to several galleries, and many artists benefitted from his personal tutelage.

In his most famous essay, 'Avant-Garde and Kitsch' (1939), Greenberg argued that the essential function of the avant-garde was to keep culture alive by resisting the negative effects of capitalism, and in doing so laid the foundations for the 'high art' versus 'low art' debate that permeated much art criticism during the second half of the twentieth century.

After the Second World War, Greenberg argued that the best avant-garde artists of the time were American rather than European. His support for Abstract Expressionism was set forth in the 1955 essay 'American-Type Painting', one of his central statements about the development of modern art. Here he commended the works of Jackson Pollock, Willem de Kooning, Barnett Newman and Clyfford Still for their emphasis on the flatness of the picture plane, a characteristic that for him represented the latest advancement in

modern art. As his 1960 essay 'Modernist Painting' explained, Greenberg saw modern art as a progression towards pure abstraction that began with the experiments of Édouard Manet and Paul Cézanne.

Greenberg's concept of formalism advocated the idea that painting should be exclusively non-representational, drawing attention solely to its own materiality. To that end he wished to see painting purged of references to anything other than itself. In 1964 he coined the term 'post-painterly abstraction' to describe a new generation of artists whose Colour Field and hard-edge paintings reflected this position. The large canvases of Morris Louis, Kenneth Noland and Jules Olitski, which are dominated by flat expanses of colour and minimal surface detail, represented the inevitable next step in the evolution of modern art.

Greenberg's ideas enjoyed wider recognition after the publication of 'Art and Culture' in 1961, an influential collection of his writings. But, while his theories influenced some younger critics, in the 1970s a new generation of both artists and critics took issue with his antagonism towards politically engaged art and emerging Postmodernist approaches. Nevertheless, the extent of Greenberg's influence upon modern art remains unsurpassed.

David Trigg

STUDY AFTER VELÁZQUEZ'S PORTRAIT OF POPE INNOCENT X
FRANCIS BACON (1909–92)

the 30-second artwork

A screaming pope grasps his gilded throne as if caught in the midst of some apocalyptic disaster. The figure's terror-stricken face appears to be dissolving amid a mass of violent, vertical brushstrokes. The bright shades of purple and yellow used for the papal vestments and throne add to the energy of the surreal composition. Bacon based this painting on a portrait of Pope Innocent X painted by the Spanish artist Velázquez in 1650. Historically, artists have always made copies of other artists' works as a creative exercise, but here Bacon subverts Velázquez's pope, transforming him from a powerful and confident figure into a vulnerable and helpless one. The pope's expression was famously inspired by a powerful cinematic image – a close-up shot of a screaming, bespectacled nurse from Sergei Eisenstein's film *Battleship Potemkin* (1925). That same scream appears throughout Bacon's work: on the faces of businessmen, politicians and writhing semi-human figures. It epitomizes the horror the world felt in the wake of the Nazi Holocaust after the Second World War. A passionately committed painter, Bacon was one of the most successful British artists of the twentieth century, producing many powerful images of traumatized humanity during the post-war period.

3-SECOND SKETCH
Surrealism, Soviet film, Old Master painting and the horrors of war all influenced this painting, which is one of Bacon's most celebrated works.

3-MINUTE STUDY
Although he was an atheist, Bacon was fascinated by the papal theme. He returned to the Velázquez portrait again and again, creating more than 45 variations of the seventeenth-century masterpiece during the 1950s and early 1960s. Yet Bacon, who worked exclusively from photographs and reproductions, never saw the original painting. Even when he visited Rome in 1954 he deliberately avoided visiting the Velázquez, which hangs in the Palazzo Doria Pamphilj.

DETAILS OF THE WORK
Oil on canvas, 1953
153 x 118 cm (60¼ x 46½ in)
Des Moines Art Center, USA

3-SECOND BIOGRAPHIES
DIEGO VELÁZQUEZ
1599–1660
Prolific Spanish artist who became court painter for King Philip IV

SERGEI EISENSTEIN
1898–1948
Soviet film director whose 1925 film *Battleship Potemkin* was considered by Bacon to be a catalyst for his paintings

DAVID SYLVESTER
1924–2001
Eminent British art critic and leading authority on Francis Bacon's work

30-SECOND TEXT
David Trigg

An atmosphere of nightmarish horror haunts this enigmatic portrait of a screaming pope.

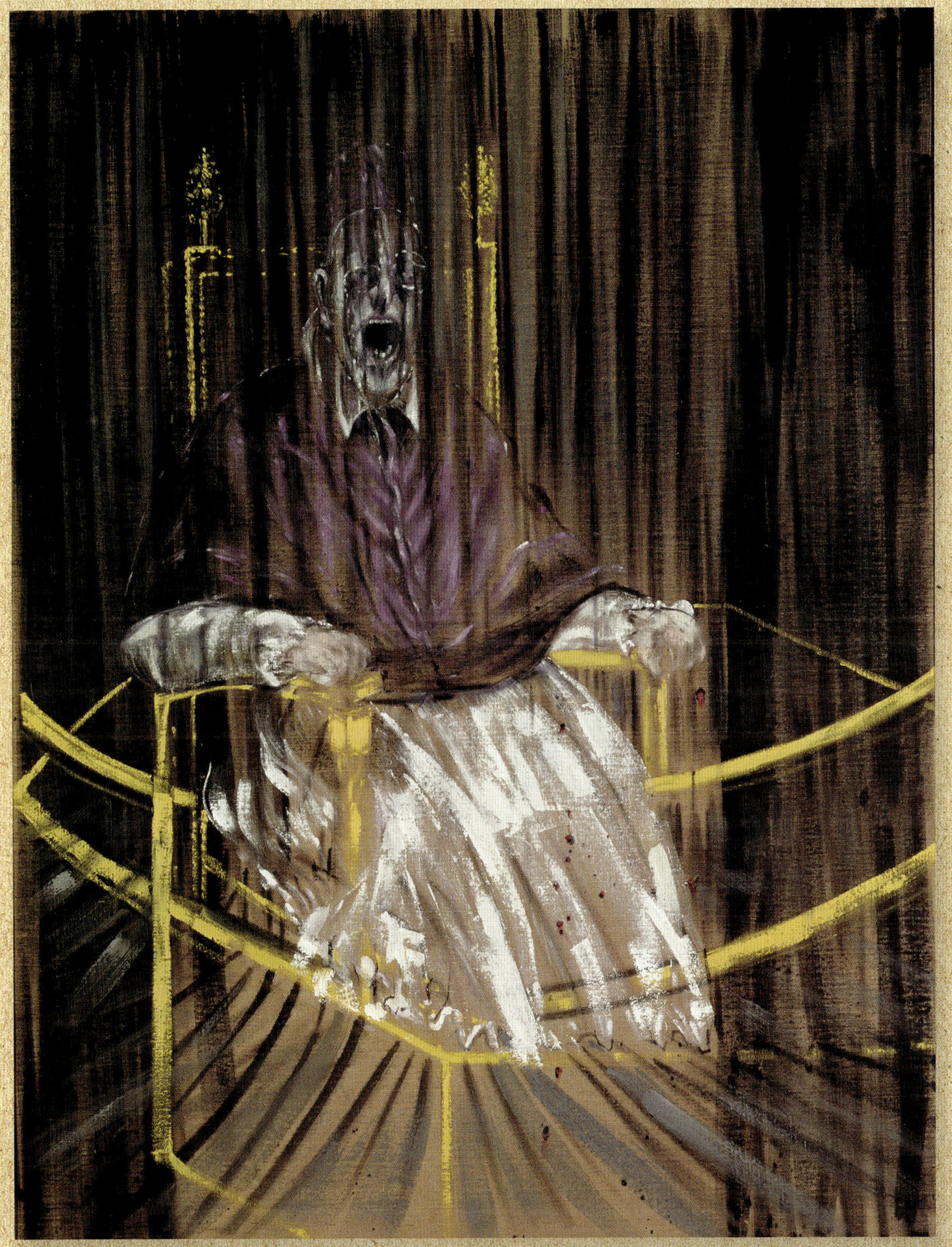

FLAG
JASPER JOHNS (1930–)

the 30-second artwork

When this painting was made, American art was dominated by Abstract Expressionism. Johns, however, rejected the notion that painting should be about self-expression, choosing instead to paint everyday symbols such as flags, targets and numbers. These banal subjects were chosen for their overfamiliarity, yet the artist's unconventional technique was anything but familiar. Instead of oil paint, *Flag* is made from strips of newspaper dipped in encaustic – a mixture of coloured pigment and molten wax. The image, comprised of three panels, has a thick, textured surface through which snippets of random news stories are just visible. Johns wanted to provoke viewers to re-examine the ubiquitous image of the American flag, believing that they should determine the meaning of his work for themselves. Despite its simple, geometric design, *Flag* contains a complex web of associations and meanings; for some the symbol evokes national pride and freedom, while for others it represents imperialism and oppression. The contradictions inherent in the stars and stripes became an important theme for Johns, who made more than forty works based on the flag's design. Johns had a significant influence on the development of American art, particularly Pop Art, a movement he anticipated by several years.

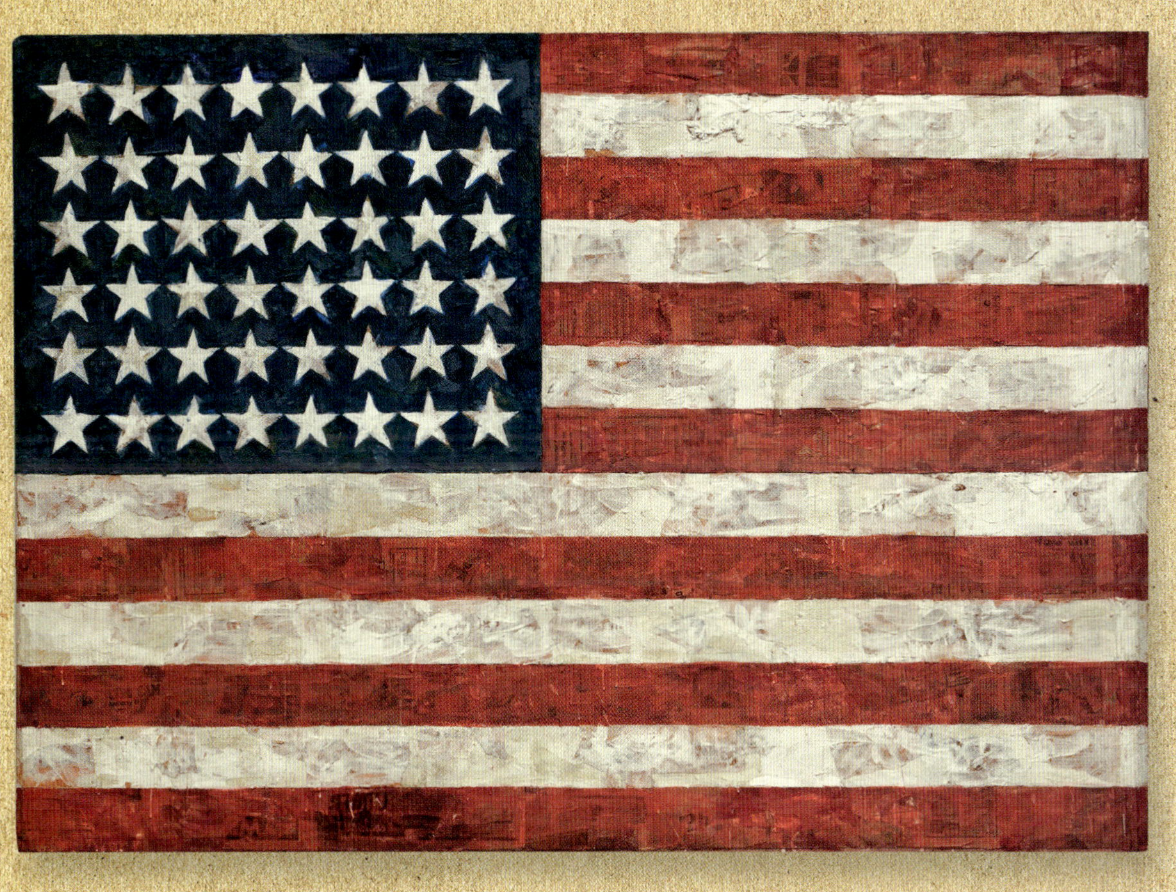

the 30-second artwork

Caro's industrial-like construction of metal plates and beams stretches out across the gallery floor. The bright red structure exemplifies a radical new development in British sculpture that the artist pioneered in the 1960s. Caro, who had worked as an assistant to Henry Moore in the early 1950s, found that clay was unsatisfactory for the type of abstract work he wanted to make. Inspired by the welded metal sculptures of the American artist David Smith, he began to experiment with manufactured, industrial materials not traditionally associated with sculpture. He found that steel and aluminium allowed him to convey a sense of balance and tension in ways that could not be achieved with other media. The resulting sculptures were entirely abstract, without reference to anything other than themselves. Working intuitively, Caro built *Early One Morning* piece by piece, guided by the wish to form harmonious relationships between each element. Unlike painting or figurative sculpture, there is no single point of focus here; viewers can walk around the piece and approach it from any angle. With works like this, Caro challenged the notion of what a sculpture could be and, by removing the traditional pedestal and placing them directly on the floor, successfully liberated his work from the baggage of art history.

3-SECOND SKETCH
This large, brightly painted sculpture made from welded steel and aluminium contributed to the transformation of British sculpture in the 1960s.

3-MINUTE STUDY
Caro built this sculpture in the garage of his London home. It grew so long that the garage doors had to be kept permanently open until it was finished. Originally, it was painted green but, at the suggestion of his wife, Caro repainted it red. The sculpture contains no references to the external world but is named after an English folk song, alluding to the fact that Caro often compared creating sculpture to composing music.

DETAILS OF THE WORK
Painted steel and aluminium, 1962
289.6 x 619.8 x 335.3 cm
(114 x 244 x 132 in)
Tate Collection, London

3-SECOND BIOGRAPHIES
HENRY MOORE
1898–1986
British sculptor celebrated for his monumental, semi-abstract bronze sculptures

DAVID SMITH
1906–65
American abstract sculptor and painter, best known for creating large welded-steel sculptures

30-SECOND TEXT
David Trigg

This landmark sculpture established Caro as one of Britain's leading young artists.

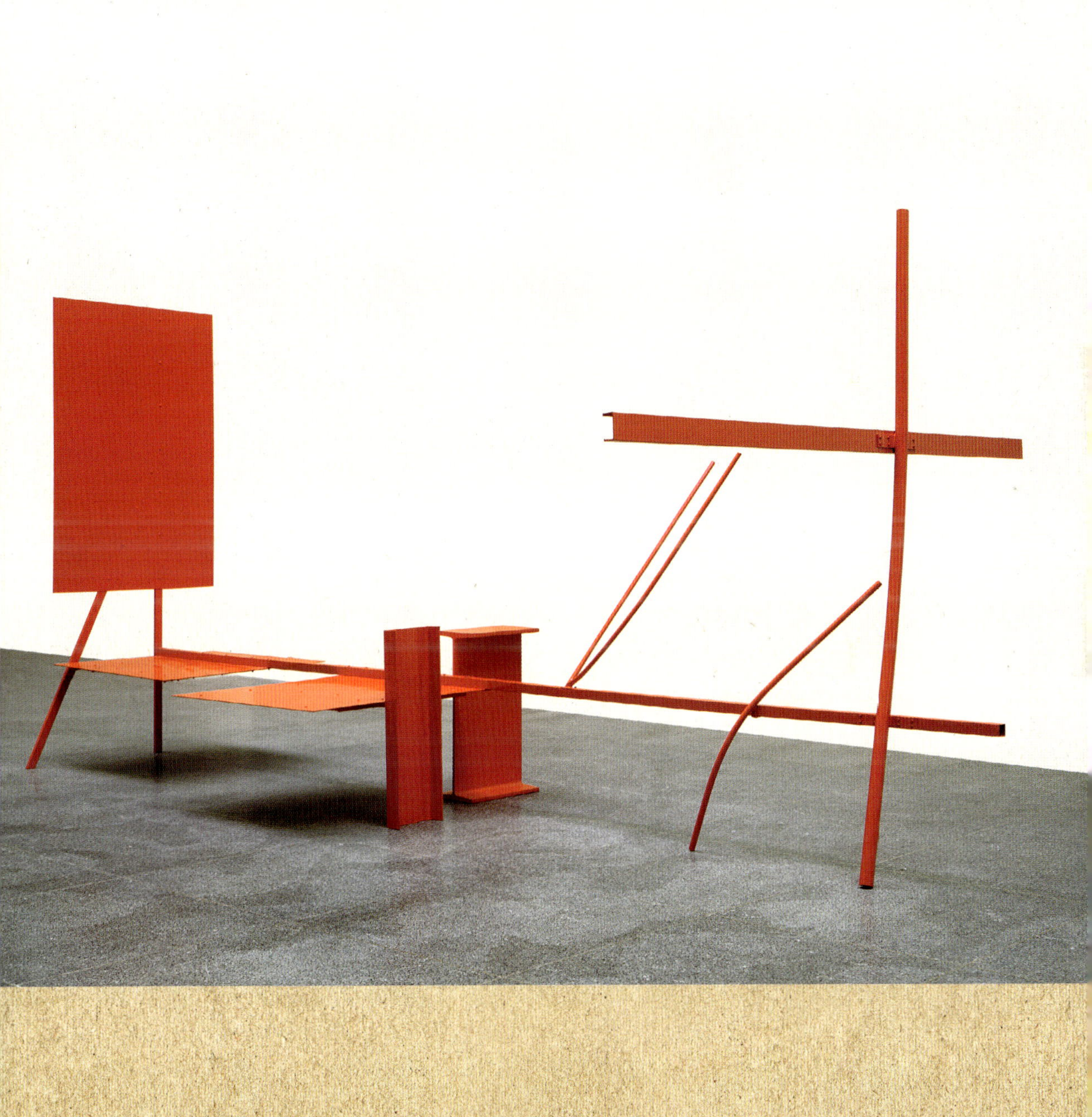

BRILLO BOX (SOAP PADS)
ANDY WARHOL (1928–87)

the 30-second artwork

Warhol's multiple *Brillo Boxes* mimic the bright, bold packaging of a commercial product. They were first exhibited at Eleanor Ward's Stable Gallery in New York alongside other replica grocery cartons featuring well-known brands. Gerard Malanga assisted Warhol in the creation of the plywood facsimiles at the artist's New York studio known as The Factory. Here they used Warhol's trademark technique of silkscreen printing, a process that allows for multiple copies of the same image to be stencilled quickly and easily. Warhol was one of the most important figures in the first generation of American Pop artists, taking popular culture, mass media and consumerism as his subjects. A painter, graphic artist and filmmaker, he became a cult figure during the 1960s and has influenced generations of artists. His Brillo boxes are virtually indistinguishable from the originals designed by commercial artist James Harvey. In this way the sculptures raise fundamental questions about the nature of art and how works of art can be distinguished from identical-looking objects not intended as art. Like much of the artist's work they remain an enigma; with no explanation from Warhol himself, viewers are left to wonder whether they represent a celebration of consumer culture or a subtle critique of it.

3-SECOND SKETCH

Warhol's life-size replicas of the Brillo Company's commercial packaging are made from plywood and are painted using the artist's signature silkscreen technique.

3-MINUTE STUDY

Warhol shocked the art world in 1962 with his paintings of Campbell's Soup cans. The *Brillo Boxes* and related sculptures were the culmination of his early interest in American consumer goods. Brillo, like Campbell's, was a compelling symbol of post-war consumerism and, to emphasize this, Warhol displayed the boxes stacked up as if in a supermarket warehouse. In doing so he transformed these mundane consumer objects into icons of contemporary culture.

DETAILS OF THE WORK

Synthetic polymer paint and silkscreen ink on wood, 1964
43.3 x 43.2 x 36.5 cm
(17⅛ x 17 x 14 in)
MoMA, New York

3-SECOND BIOGRAPHIES

ELEANOR WARD
1911–84
Art dealer who hosted Warhol's first solo Pop Art exhibition at her New York gallery in 1962

JAMES HARVEY
1929–65
Commercial artist who designed the striking Brillo logo appropriated by Warhol

GERARD MALANGA
1943–
American poet and photographer who was one of Warhol's closest associates during the 1960s

30-SECOND TEXT
David Trigg

*Celebrated as a painter, Warhol made few sculptures, but his **Brillo Boxes** are among Pop Art's best known works.*

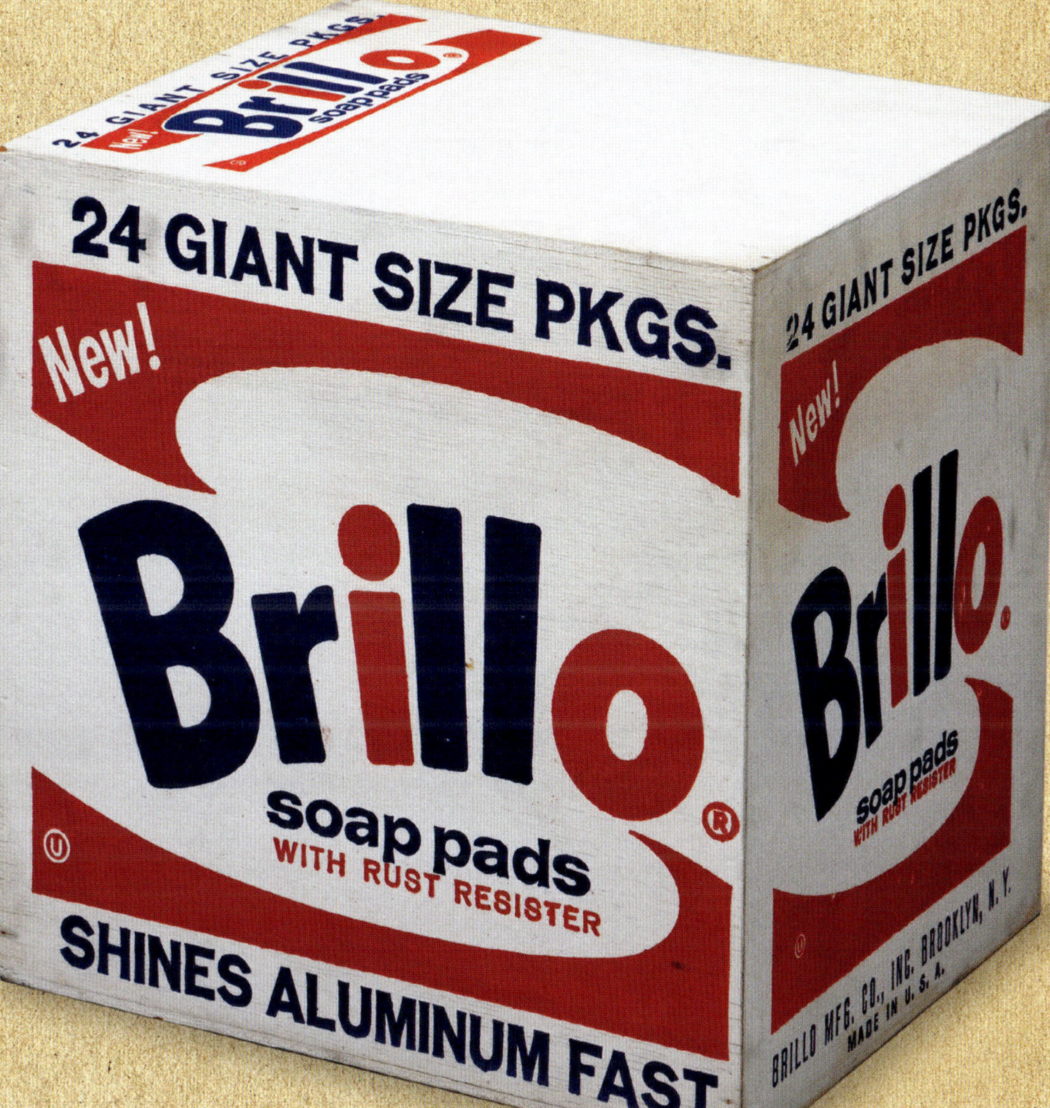

24 GIANT SIZE PKGS.
New!
Brillo.
soap pads
WITH RUST RESISTER
SHINES ALUMINUM FAST
24 GIANT SIZE PKGS.
New!
Brillo.
soap pads
WITH RUST RESISTER
BRILLO MFG. CO., INC. BROOKLYN, N. Y.
MADE IN U. S. A.
24 GIANT SIZE PKGS.
Brillo.
soap pads

CATARACT 3
BRIDGET RILEY (1931–)

the 30-second artwork

Waves of red, turquoise and grey undulate diagonally across a white canvas in a repeating pattern. The colours appear to vibrate, evoking a subtle sense of movement. Visual illusions like this are a defining characteristic of Riley's paintings. Her fascination with optical effects stems from an interest in the work of Georges Seurat, whose figurative paintings were created using thousands of small dots of coloured paint (a technique known as Pointillism), which relied on the viewer's eyes and brain to blend them from a distance into a full range of tones. As with Seurat, nothing in Riley's paintings is left to chance. With painstaking precision she carefully plans out her compositions on paper before committing them to canvas. Riley, whose career has spanned six decades, was a leading exponent of the 1960s art movement Op Art, which used the interplay of line, shape and pattern to create the illusion of movement on a static canvas. She became well known for working in this style after her first exhibition at Victor Musgrave's influential London gallery. In fact, in the 1960s her paintings became so popular they began to influence the worlds of graphic design, fashion and interior design. Those who plagiarized the artist's work, however, were sued for copyright infringement.

DETAILS OF THE WORK
Emulsion PVA on linen, 1967
221.9 x 222.9 cm (87¼ x 87¾ in)
British Council Collection

3-SECOND BIOGRAPHIES
GEORGES SEURAT
1859–91
French Post-Impressionist painter whose innovative Pointillist style has influenced Riley's work

VICTOR MUSGRAVE
1919–84
Leading British art dealer and founder of Gallery One, who in 1962 staged Riley's first solo exhibition

30-SECOND TEXT
David Trigg

This painting appears machine-made but in fact is painstakingly painted by hand.

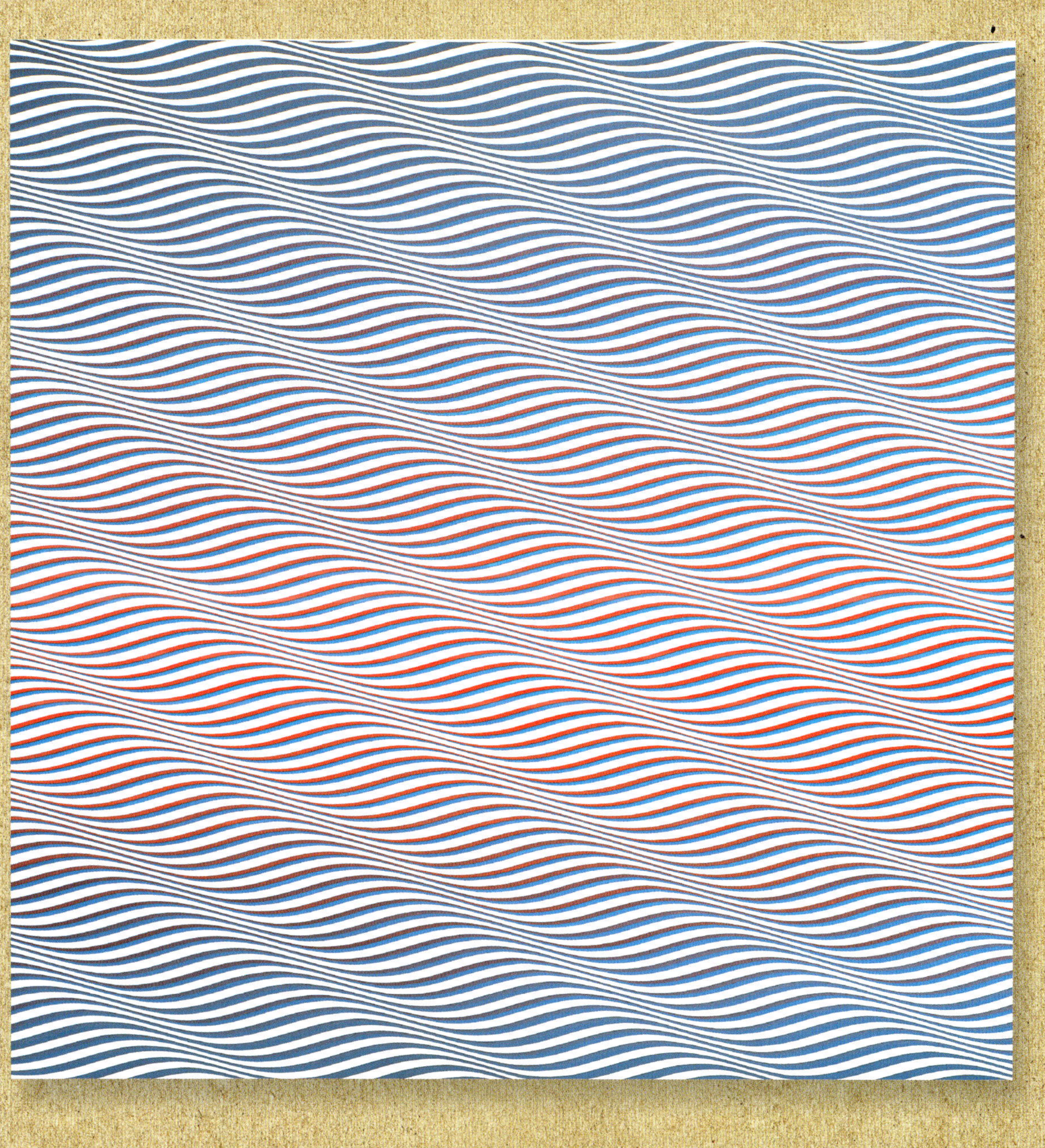

THE WHITE DISEASE
MARLENE DUMAS (1953–)

the 30-second artwork

This large portrait, based on a medical photograph, depicts an anonymous South African woman disfigured by a horrible skin disease. The patient's face, painted with thin layers of translucent paint, is frail and pallid; her blue eyes stare out from the canvas with a haunted, hopeless expression. As with many of Dumas's paintings and drawings, the figure is set against a neutral backdrop, isolated and alone. Race, gender and suffering are recurring themes in Dumas's figurative paintings, which have featured celebrities, models, babies and, as here, anonymous faces. Dumas distances herself from her subjects through the use of found images and newspaper photographs, yet personal memories and experiences are always the starting point for her art. Here, the painting's title refers not to the woman's condition but to the political unrest in the artist's native South Africa under the brutal apartheid regime, and also to Western culture portraying white as the norm. Growing up during apartheid in the 1960s and '70s, Dumas experienced first-hand the institutionalized discrimination and racial segregation that favoured white citizens and repressed the black majority in South Africa. For Dumas, the identity of the woman is irrelevant; the uncomfortable image is used as a metaphor for racism in society as a destructive disease.

Marlene Dumas's enigmatic paintings challenge the traditional genre of portraiture by addressing wider societal issues.

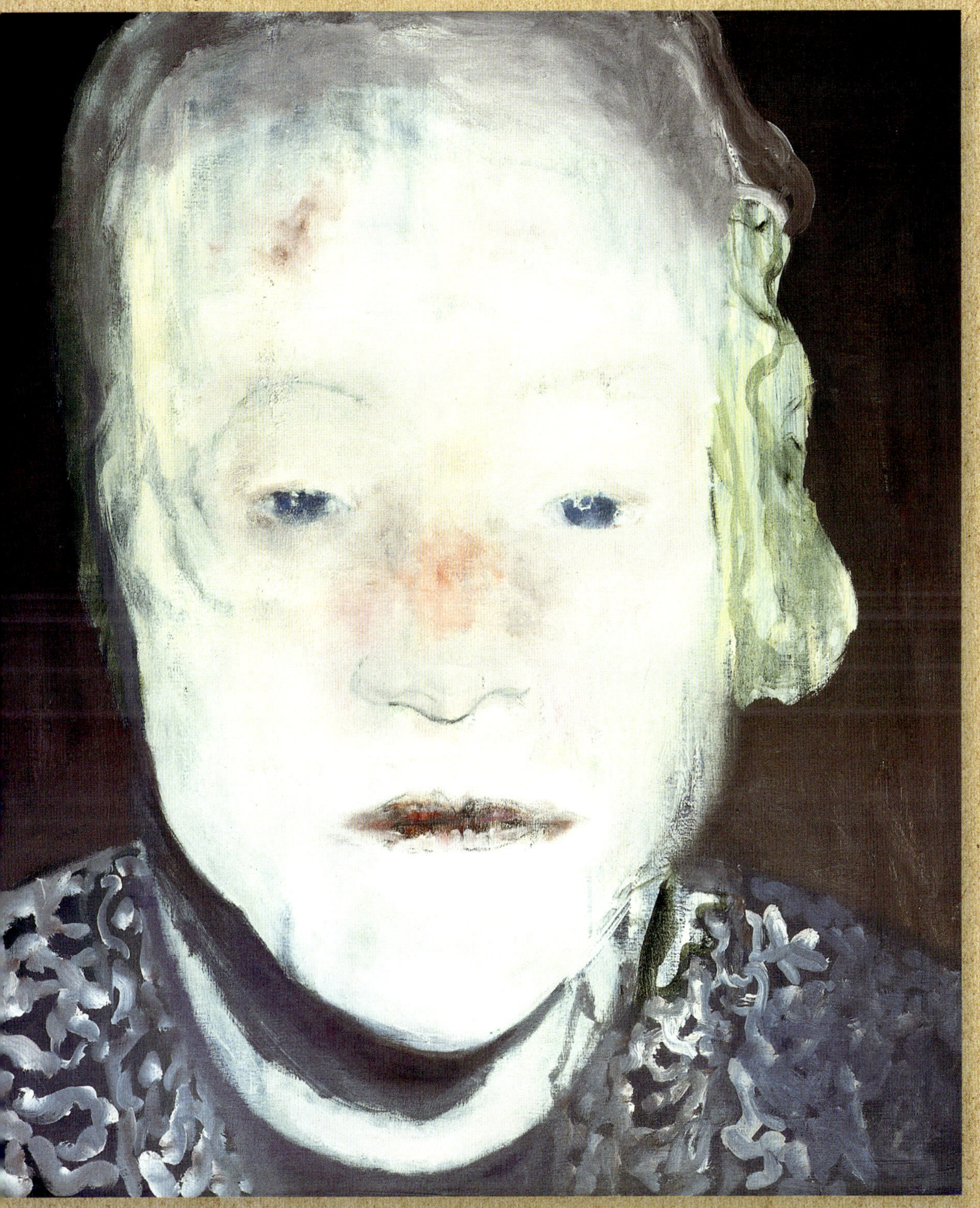

LINE OF CONTROL
SUBODH GUPTA (1964–)

the 30-second artwork

A colossal mushroom cloud

formed from shiny utensils dominates the gallery. Dwarfing its viewers, Gupta's imposing sculpture comprises thousands of stainless steel vessels from his native India, including pots, pans and the ubiquitous tiffin lunch boxes used across the subcontinent. Such items represent domesticity and daily routine but are also symbolic of a country that has experienced rapid economic expansion. The artist's strategy of using off-the-shelf cooking equipment recalls the 'ready-made' sculptures of Marcel Duchamp, which often incorporated commercially produced objects. Subverting the original function of these products, Gupta uses them as sculptural material to create a single, gigantic metal object. The work's title refers to contested borders, such as that between India and Pakistan, a military control line dividing the Jammu and Kashmir region. In 1999 the two nations were on the brink of an atomic conflict; leading to apocalyptic predictions regarding the potential destruction and loss of life. With this sculpture Gupta's use of ordinary, everyday items alludes to the cataclysmic impact upon daily life that would result if the full force of any nation's nuclear arsenals were ever unleashed.

DETAILS OF THE WORK
Stainless steel utensils, stainless steel and steel structure, 2008
h 10 x w 10 x d 10 m
(h 33 x w 33 x d 33 ft)
Kiran Nadar Museum of Art, New Delhi

3-SECOND BIOGRAPHIES
KIRAN NADAR
1951–
Indian art collector, philanthropist and founder of the Kiran Nadar Museum of Art in New Delhi

MARCEL DUCHAMP
1887–1968
Influential French artist and pioneer of conceptual art, who believed that art should be driven by ideas

30-SECOND TEXT
David Trigg

A towering mushroom cloud created from twenty-six tons of pots and pans addresses the threat of nuclear war.

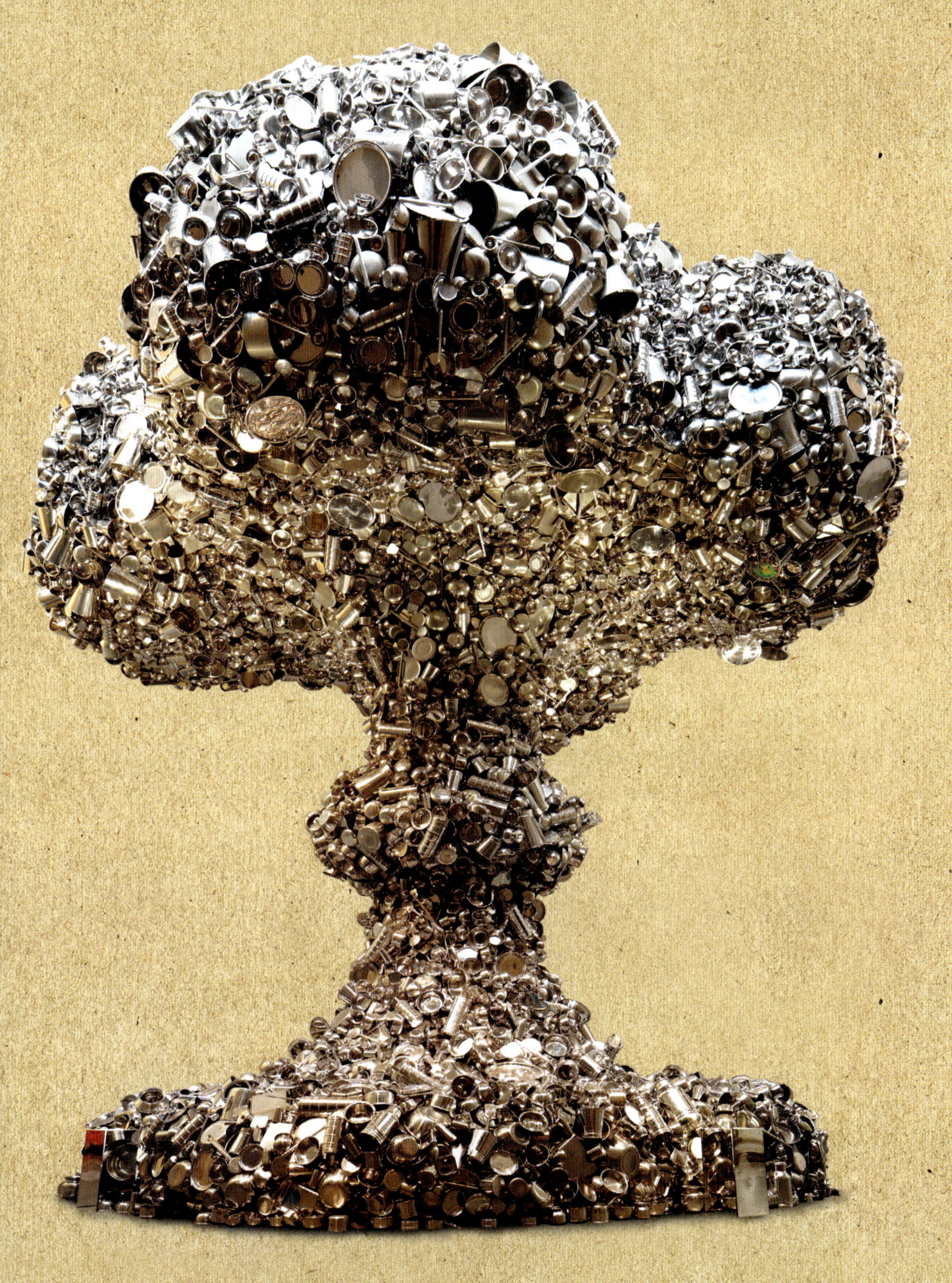

APPENDICES

RESOURCES

BOOKS

Art in Time: A World History of Styles and Movements
Noit Banai, Gauvin Alexander Bailey, Lee Beard, Lucy Bowditch et al.
(Phaidon, 2014)

Art in Renaissance Italy 1350–1500
Evelyn Welch
(Oxford University Press, 2000)

The Art of the Northern Renaissance
Craig Harbison
(Laurence King, 2012)

Painting and Experience in Fifteenth-Century Italy
Michael Baxandall
(Oxford University Press, 1988)

Beyond Caravaggio
Letizia Treves, Aidan Weston-Lewis, Gabriele Finaldi, Christian Tico Seifert, Adriaan Waiboer
(Yale University Press, 2016)

Portraiture
Shearer West
(Oxford University Press, 2004)

Art and Visual Culture 1600–1850. Academy to Avant-Garde
Emma Barker
(Tate Publishing, 2012)

Neoclassicism
David Irwin
(Phaidon, 1997)

Romanticism and Art
William Vaughan
(Thames & Hudson, 1994)

Landscape and Western Art
Malcolm Andrews
(Oxford University Press, 1999)

Pre-Raphaelites: Victorian Avant-Garde
Tim Barringer, Jason Rosenfeld, Alison Smith
(Tate Publishing, 2012)

The Painting of Modern Life: Paris in the Art of Manet and His Followers
T. J. Clark
(Princeton University Press, 1999)

English Art and Modernism 1900–1939
Charles Harrison
(Yale University Press, 1981)

Art in France, 1900–1940
Christopher Green
(Yale University Press, 2003)

Dada and Surrealism
Matthew Gale
(Phaidon, 1997)

Art Since 1900: Modernism,
Antimodernism, Postmodernism
Hal Foster, Rosalind Krauss, Yve-Alain Bois,
Benjamin H. D. Buchloh
(Thames & Hudson, 2004)

Themes in Contemporary Art
Gill Perry, Paul Wood
(Yale University Press, 2004)

The Art Book
Lee Beard, Adam Butler, Claire Van Cleave,
Diane Fortenberry, Susan Sterling
(Phaidon, new edition, 2012)

The Art of Art History: A Critical Anthology
Donald Preziosi
(Oxford University Press, 1998)

WEBSITES

Artcyclopedia
www.artcyclopedia.com

Dictionary of Art Historians
www.dictionaryofarthistorians.org

Gallerie degli Uffizi, Florence
www.uffizi.it

Musée du Louvre, Paris
www.louvre.fr

Museo del Prado, Madrid
www.museodelprado.es

Museum of Modern Art (MoMA), New York
www.moma.org

National Gallery, London
www.nationalgallery.org.uk

Routledge Encyclopedia of Modernism
www.rem.routledge.com

Web Gallery of Art
www.wga.hu

EDITOR

Lee Beard is an independent art historian and editor. He studied at the University of Manchester and the Courtauld Institute of Art, and has been a visiting lecturer at the Courtauld. He is a recognized expert on the work of the artist Ben Nicholson (1894–1982) and is editor of the Ben Nicholson Catalogue Raisonné. He has written for a range of publications focusing on modern art in Britain during the twentieth century.

CONTRIBUTORS

Maria Alambritis is an AHRC Collaborative Doctoral Award PhD candidate with the National Gallery and Birkbeck, University of London, researching nineteenth-century women art historians writing on the Italian Old Masters. She completed an interdisciplinary BA in Art History and Literature at the University of East Anglia and her Masters at the Courtauld, specializing in British Aesthetic art and art writing. Before beginning her PhD, she held roles as the HLF Arts Curatorial Trainee at Birmingham Museum and Art Gallery and as Curatorial Assistant at the Royal Academy, London.

Thomas Balfe received his MA (2009) and PhD (2014) from The Courtauld Institute of Art, University of London, where he has worked since 2010. To date, his own research has focused on sixteenth- and seventeenth-century animal, food and hunting imagery.

Simona Di Nepi is a curator and lecturer who has been Assistant Curator of Renaissance paintings at the National Gallery, London, where she curated the exhibition *Reunions: Bringing Early Italian Paintings Back Together*. She is the author of *Duccio to Leonardo: Renaissance Painting from 1250 to 1500* (National Gallery Company, 2009). She is currently Curator of Judaica at the Museum of Fine Arts, Boston.

Elena Greer is an author at the National Gallery, London where she writes about the collection's early Renaissance Italian paintings. She obtained her PhD in the history of art at the University of Nottingham and her MA at the Courtauld Institute. She has published on a variety of art-historical topics including catalogue entries on Renaissance portraiture, Venetian painting from the fourteenth to eighteenth century and Dutch painting, as well as articles on the history of collecting and display at the National Gallery, London.

Paul Harper studied at Bucks New University and has a PhD from London Metropolitan University. He has a wide range of experience in arts management and now combines research and writing with teaching the history and philosophy of art and design at Middlesex University and London Metropolitan University. Paul's research interests focus on the experience of craft practices. He was a contributing author to *The Twenty First Century Art Book* (Phaidon, 2014).

Sarah Moulden is Curator of Collections at English Heritage and a specialist in eighteenth- and early nineteenth-century British art. She completed her first degrees in Art History at the Courtauld Institute of Art. Her PhD was on the art and career of the British artist, John Sell Cotman, completed at the University of East Anglia in collaboration with Norwich Castle Museum & Art Gallery. At English Heritage, Sarah is responsible for the collections and historic interiors of Darwin's home at Down House, Eltham Palace and Ranger's House in South London.

David Trigg is an art critic and writer based in Bristol. He is a regular contributor to books on modern art, including *The Twenty First Century Art Book* (Phaidon, 2014), and has written articles and reviews for a wide range of journals and magazines, including *Art Monthly* and *ArtReview*. He has a PhD in Art History from the University of Bristol and is a member of the International Association of Art Critics.

INDEX

ACKNOWLEDGEMENTS

The publisher would like to thank the following for permission to reproduce copyright material on the following pages:

7 Rijksmuseum, Amsterdam.

8 National Gallery of Art, Washington.

9 Alamy/Heritage Image Partnership Ltd.

15 Getty Images/De Agostini.

17 Getty Images/Mondadori Portfolio.

19 Alamy/World History Archive.

21 Scala, Florence/Courtesy of the Ministero Beni e Att. Culturali.

25 Alamy/Classicpaintings.

27 Scala, Florence.

33 Getty Images/Leemage/Corbis.

35 Scala, Florence/BPK, Bildagentur fuer Kunst, Kultur und Geschichte, Berlin.

37 Alamy/Granger Historical Picture Archive.

39 Bridgeman Images/© Staatliche Kunstsammlungen Dresden.

41 Getty/VCG Wilson/Corbis.

43 Bridgeman Images/Galleria degli Uffizi, Florence, Tuscany, Italy.

44 Shutterstock/Georgios Kollidas.

51 Getty Images/Leemage/Corbis.

53 Alamy/Artexplorer.

55 Bridgeman Images/Kunsthistorisches Museum, Vienna, Austria.

56 Rijksmuseum, Amsterdam.

61 Bridgeman Images/Prado, Madrid, Spain.

63 Rijksmuseum, Amsterdam.

65 National Gallery of Art, Washington.

71 Alamy/World History Archive.

73 Yale University Art Gallery.

75 Scala, Florence/White Images.

77 Bridgeman Images/Louvre, Paris, France.

79 Alamy/Classicpaintings.

81 Bridgeman Images/Hamburger Kunsthalle, Hamburg, Germany.

82 Yale University Art Gallery.

85 Alamy/Heritage Image Partnership Ltd.

87 Alamy/Heritage Image Partnership Ltd.

93 Bridgeman Images/Birmingham Museums and Art Gallery.

95 National Gallery of Art, Washington.

97 Alamy/Granger Historical Picture Archive.

103 Getty Images/VCG Wilson/Corbis.

105 J. Paul Getty Museum, Los Angeles. Digital image courtesy of the Getty's Open Content Program.

107 Getty Images.

113 © Succession H. Matisse/DACS 2018. Image: Bridgeman Images/The Barnes Foundation, Philadelphia, Pennsylvania, USA.

115 Getty Images/Mondadori Portfolio.

117 The Metropolitan Museum of Art.

119 © ADAGP, Paris and DACS, London 2018. Image: Alamy/Heritage Image Partnership Ltd.

121 AKG Images.

122 Getty Images/Lusha Nelson/Condé Nast.

125 © Succession Picasso/DACS, London 2018. Image: © Tate, London 2017.

127 © BOWNESS. Image: National Galleries Scotland. Purchased with support from the Heritage Lottery Fund, the Art Fund and the Henry Moore Foundation 1999.

129 © Banco de México Diego Rivera Frida Kahlo Museums Trust, Mexico, D.F/DACS 2018. Image: Alamy/Granger Historical Picture Archive.

135 © The Pollock-Krasner Foundation ARS, NY and DACS, London 2018. Image: Bridgeman Images/Peggy Guggenheim Foundation, Venice, Italy.

136 Getty Images/Kenn Bisio/The Denver Post.

139 © The Estate of Francis Bacon. All rights reserved. DACS 2018. Image: Bridgeman Images/Des Moines Art Center.

141 © Jasper Johns/VAGA, New York/DACS, London 2018. Image: Scala, Florence/Copyright Digital image, The Museum of Modern Art, New York.

143 © Courtesy of Barford Sculptures Ltd. Photo: John Riddy.

145 © 2018 The Andy Warhol Foundation for the Visual Arts, Inc /Licensed by DACS, London. Image: Scala, Florence/Copyright Digital image, The Museum of Modern Art, New York.

147 © Bridget Riley 2017. All rights reserved.

149 © Marlene Dumas. Courtesy David Zwirner New York/London.

151 Installation view 'Altermodern Tate Triennial 2009', London, England. Courtesy the artist and Hauser & Wirth. Photo: Mike Bruce.

All reasonable efforts have been made to trace copyright holders and to obtain their permission for the use of copyright material. The publisher apologizes for any errors or omissions in the list above and will gratefully incorporate any corrections in future reprints if notified.